VEGETABLES

Design and Typesetting: Alice Leroy
Editorial Collaboration: Estérelle Payany

Project Coordinator, FERRANDI Paris: Audrey Janet
Chefs, FERRANDI Paris: Jérémie Barnay, Stéphane Jakic,
and Frédéric Lesourd
Technical Assistant: Mae Alfeche

Editor: Clélia Ozier-Lafontaine

English Edition
Editorial Director: Kate Mascaro
Editor: Helen Adedotun
Translated from the French by Carmella Moreau (recipes)
and Ansley Evans (introductory text)
Copyediting and Additional Translation: Wendy Sweetser
Proofreading: Nicole Foster
Indexing: JMS/Chris Bell
Production: Louisa Hanifi-Morard and Christelle Lemonnier
Color Separation: IGS-CP L'Isle d'Espagnac
Printed in China by Toppan Leefung

Simultaneously published in French as
Légumes : Recettes et techniques d'une école d'excellence
© Flammarion, S.A., Paris, 2020
English-language edition
© Flammarion, S.A., Paris, 2020

20 21 22 3 2 1
ISBN: 978-2-08-151342-6
Legal Deposit: 11/2020

FERRANDI

PARIS

VEGETABLES

FLEXITARIAN RECIPES AND TECHNIQUES
FROM THE FERRANDI SCHOOL OF CULINARY ARTS

Photography by Rina Nurra

Flammarion

PREFACE

For one hundred years, **FERRANDI Paris** has taught all of the culinary disciplines to students from around the world. Following the success of our two previous works published by Flammarion—a comprehensive, didactic, and delicious compendium of French pâtisserie recipes and a volume focusing specifically on the art of chocolate making—it is time to shine the spotlight on vegetables. Edible plants come in an extraordinary range of different varieties and they deserve to play a starring, rather than a supporting, role on our plates.

Although appreciation for vegetables is on the rise in many countries, plants have long been neglected in traditional French cuisine. An early staple of the human diet, vegetables, along with cereal grains, were considered less noble than meat and thus featured rarely in French culinary texts and on haute-cuisine menus. But the sheer variety of the vegetable world—from carrots, potatoes, leeks, and cabbage, to Jerusalem artichokes, pumpkins, and mushrooms, to name but a few—offers inspiration and infinite possibilities for chefs.

Both traditional skills and creative innovation lie at the heart of **FERRANDI Paris's** teaching philosophy. We maintain a balance between the two through strong ties to the professional world, making our school a leading institution in the field. That is why this book not only provides delicious recipes in which vegetables are given pride of place, in both vegetarian and non-vegetarian dishes, but also demonstrates fundamental techniques and shares expert advice. Anyone who wishes to explore the inspiring world of vegetables, whether it be at home or in a professional kitchen, will find this volume invaluable.

I extend my warmest thanks to those members of **FERRANDI Paris** who have made this book a reality, particularly Audrey Janet, who coordinated the project, and Jérémie Barnay, Stéphane Jakic, and Frédéric Lesourd, head chefs at the school, who have generously shared their expertise, adeptly combining technical skills and creativity in order to show us the rich culinary potential of the vegetable garden. And for those with an aversion to certain vegetables—no matter your age—we hope this book will surprise you and inspire you to change your mind!

Bruno de Monte
Director of FERRANDI Paris

CONTENTS

106 RECIPES

298 APPENDIXES

INTRODUCTION

A Portrait of **FERRANDI Paris**

In its one-hundred-year history, **FERRANDI Paris** has earned an international reputation as one of the premier culinary and hospitality schools in France. Since its inception, the school—hailed by the press as "the Harvard of gastronomy"—has trained generations of groundbreaking chefs and entrepreneurs who have left their mark in the industry worldwide. Whether at its historic campus in the Saint-Germain-des-Prés neighborhood of Paris, its campus in Bordeaux, or its soon-to-open sites in Rennes and Dijon, **FERRANDI Paris** is dedicated to world-class teaching with the aim of training future leaders in the culinary and pastry arts, hotel and restaurant management, and hospitality entrepreneurship.

Founded in 1920 by the Paris Île-de-France Regional Chamber of Commerce and Industry, **FERRANDI Paris** is the only school in France to offer the full range of degree and certification programs in the culinary and hospitality professions, from vocational training to master's degree level, in addition to international programs. The school takes pride in its 98 percent exam pass rate, the highest in France for degrees and certifications in the sector. No matter the level, a **FERRANDI Paris** education is rigorous and combines a mastery of fundamental techniques with an emphasis on innovation, management, and entrepreneurial skills, as well as hands-on experience in a professional environment.

Strong Ties to the Professional World

A space for discovery, inspiration, and exchange—where the culinary arts mingle with science, technology, and innovation—**FERRANDI Paris** brings together the biggest names in the sector to discuss and shape the future of the hospitality industry and push the boundaries of culinary creativity. The school trains 2,200 apprentices and students each year, in addition to three hundred international students of more than thirty nationalities and two thousand adults who come to the school to perfect their skills or to change careers. The hundred instructors at the school are all highly qualified. Several have received prominent culinary awards and distinctions, such as the

Meilleurs Ouvriers de France title (Best Craftsmen of France), and all have at least ten years' experience of working in the culinary field at prestigious establishments in France and abroad.

To give students maximum opportunities and the chance to connect with other fields and the greater global community, the school has formed collaborative partnerships with several other institutions. In France, partner schools include the ESCP Europe Business School, AgroParis Tech, and the Institut Français de la Mode. Overseas, the school collaborates with, among others, Johnson and Wales University in the United States, the ITHQ tourism and hotel management school in Canada, the Hong Kong Polytechnic University, and the Institute for Tourism Studies in China. Since theory and practice go hand in hand, and because **FERRANDI Paris** strives for excellence in teaching, students also have the chance to participate in a number of official events through

partnerships with several leading culinary associations in France, including Maîtres Cuisiniers de France, Société des Meilleurs Ouvriers de France, Euro-Toques, and more. In addition, the school offers numerous prestigious professional competitions and prizes, giving students plenty of opportunities to demonstrate their skills and knowledge. A dedicated ambassador of French culture, every year it draws students from around the world. It is a member of the French Interministerial Tourism Council, the Strategic Committee of Atout France (the French tourism development agency), and the Conférence des Formations d'Excellence au Tourisme (CFET), a group of institutions in France offering top-quality training in tourism-related fields.

Extensive Savoir Faire
FERRANDI Paris's expertise, combining practice and close collaboration with professionals in the field, has been shared in two previous volumes—one devoted to French pâtisserie and the other to the specialized art of chocolate making—intended for both professional chefs and amateur cooks. Following the success of these two books—*Pâtisserie* received a Gourmand World Cookbook award—**FERRANDI Paris** has now turned its attention to the vegetable. Incredibly diverse, vegetables require an extensive repertoire of cooking techniques, as even staples like carrots, potatoes, and leeks

can be prepared and served in a wide variety of ways. In this latest volume, the school's teachers have put their technical skills and creativity to work to demonstrate the enormous culinary potential of the vegetable garden.

Vegetables—A World of Edible Plants to Explore
When compared to meat, the possibilities offered by vegetables are far more multifarious. The different plants we consume offer an immeasurable array of flavor sensations, including sweet (onions and leeks), earthy (beets), leafy (spinach and lettuce), aniseed (fennel), and cooly refreshing (cucumber). They also have a variety of textures ranging from crisp and crunchy when raw, to mellow and creamy when cooked. Although vegetables are often relegated to the role of a side or accompaniment to a main dish, they deserve to be appreciated in their own right. In this book, the talented **FERRANDI Paris** chefs invite you to explore the vegetable world and the myriad ways in which so many humble plants can delight our taste buds, either on their own or combined with meat, fish, or seafood. You will learn how to master not only preparation techniques, such as specific cuts and cooking methods, but also explore sophisticated and creative ways to draw out and enhance the natural characteristics of individual vegetable families. We hope you will find inspiration on this delicious—and often surprising—vegetal journey of discovery.

VEGETABLES:
THE ESSENTIALS

What is a vegetable?

The word "vegetable" is not a technical botanical term but rather a culinary distinction for edible plants that humans consume as food. There is no other defining characteristic, which explains the incredible diversity of shapes, textures, and flavors among the plants we call vegetables, whether it be their roots, bulbs, leaves, flowers, fruits, or seeds that we eat. The one thing all vegetables have in common is their capacity to delight our senses. Although we often categorize edible mushrooms as vegetables, they are not part of the plant kingdom as vegetables are, but have a classification of their own, namely fungi. The same goes for seaweed, which is technically not a plant but a type of algae.

How are vegetables classified?

There are two main classifications: by botanical plant family and according to the part of the plant we eat.

Botanical classifications

The plants we consume as vegetables belong to over twenty plant families. However, many garden vegetables can be grouped into the following ten families (non-exhaustive list):
• **Apiaceae**, or **Umbelliferae**, commonly known as the carrot or parsley family, includes carrots, celery, chervil, fennel, and parsnips, as well as a number of herbs and spices such as parsley, cilantro, lovage, and cumin.
• **Asteraceae**, or **Compositae**, the sunflower family, includes artichokes, cardoons, Jerusalem artichokes, endives, chicory, salsify, and lettuce.
• **Brassicaceae**, or **Cruciferae**, the cabbage family, encompasses all cruciferous vegetables, including cabbage, cauliflower, and broccoli, as well as certain leafy greens such as kale, arugula, and watercress.
• **Amaranthaceae**, the amaranth family of flowering plants, which contains the former goosefoot family Chenopodiaceae, includes beets, spinach, and chard.
• **Cucurbitaceae**, commonly called cucurbits or the squash or gourd family, includes pumpkins, summer and winter squash, and cucumbers.
• **Fabaceae**, or **Leguminosae**, also known as the legume, pea, or bean family, counts among its members peas, green beans, and legumes such as chickpeas and lentils.
• **Amaryllidaceae**, the onion or allium family, includes garlic, shallots, onions, and leeks.
• **Solanaceae**, also known as the nightshade family, comprises eggplants, potatoes, tomatoes, peppers, chilis, and more.

This classification by family is often complex for non-botanists to understand, as it groups together a wide variety of vegetables with different forms and flavors, requiring different preparation techniques. In this volume, only the Cucurbitaceae and Brassicaceae families—in other words, gourds and cruciferous vegetables—have their own

chapters. The other chapters have been organized according to the second type of classification explained below.

Classification by the part eaten

Vegetables can also be classified according to the part we eat, such as roots (carrots, beets), leaves (spinach, lettuce), tubers (potatoes), fruits (tomatoes, eggplants), bulbs (garlic, onions), stems (asparagus), seeds (peas, beans), and even flowers (artichokes, broccoli). This classification has been used for the organization of most of the chapters in this book, as it is more appropriate from a culinary standpoint.

Fruit or vegetable?

In culinary terms, the line that separates a vegetable from a fruit can be blurry. Some produce that we think of as being vegetables—such as zucchini, eggplants, and tomatoes—are technically fruits. To confuse matters even more, some plants that we treat as fruits—such as rhubarb—are actually vegetables. Botany and cuisine are not always in complete accord as, botanically speaking, the category "vegetable" does not exist, unlike "fruit," which is the edible organ of flowering plants.

Different farming and gardening methods

Organic or conventional? Integrated, permaculture, or intensive? In greenhouses or open fields? There are many

ways to grow vegetables and there is much debate as to the best way to feed the planet. For cooks, the most important things to consider are:
• **Freshness:** buying locally produced vegetables that have traveled as short a distance as possible is the easiest way to guarantee freshness.
• **Flavor:** flavor will depend on the variety and can vary according to how the vegetable is grown. As a general rule, vegetables that are harvested ripe and in season will taste the best.
• **Root-to-stem potential:** so that all parts can be used, including leafy tops and peel, vegetables from organic or integrated producers are best. Ensure that they are thoroughly washed.

Selecting vegetables at their best

As a general rule, the fresher the vegetable, the better it will taste. However, there are rare exceptions, such as chervil root, which is at its best after being stored for several weeks. Signs of freshness include firmness, a vibrant color, and no blemishes or wilted leaves that indicate vegetables are damaged or past their prime. Cooking vegetables as soon as possible after they have been harvested typically yields superior flavor and nutrition.

Preparation

It is essential to wash and dry vegetables thoroughly to remove dirt or grit and any surface bacteria. To limit vitamin loss (especially vitamins B and C), avoid soaking your vegetables in water for long periods. Several quick immersions are better, especially for leafy vegetables and salad greens. Peeled and cut vegetables should be kept in the refrigerator and consumed quickly to avoid nutrient loss and discoloration. **Note:** Certain vegetables (such as avocados, artichokes, parsnips, Jerusalem artichokes, kohlrabi, and salsify) oxidize and turn brown quickly once they have been peeled or cut, so they should be tossed in a bowl with lemon juice or immersed in cold water with a little lemon juice or vinegar added to prevent discoloration. Cutting vegetables into equal-sized pieces (see cutting techniques pp. 52–85) allows for even cooking, but keep in mind that smaller or thinner cuts expose vegetables to more air, resulting in greater vitamin and mineral loss.

Cooking

Some vegetables can be eaten both raw and cooked, while others, such as potatoes, must be cooked to make them more palatable and digestible. While any type of cooking destroys some of a vegetable's nutrients and enzymes, it is also beneficial as harmful bacteria are killed and, depending

on the cooking method, can enhance the value of other nutrients. Cooking can also concentrate flavors but keep in mind that long cooking times, cooking at high temperatures, or boiling in large quantities of water can be particularly detrimental to nutrients. Steaming, boiling, braising, and roasting, along with other techniques, are all explained in this book (see cooking methods pp. 86–105).

Zero waste

Respecting our vegetables means using every part of them rather than throwing trimmings away. Although we tend to eat only certain parts of a vegetable, what is left can be used advantageously in other recipes.
• **Hearty greens:** In the south of France, it is customary to remove the tough stems of chard and only eat the leaves, but in Lyon, the white stems are more appreciated than the leaves. The best solution is to use both, in different ways and in different recipes, such as adding the stems to a gratin or soup. Similarly, avoid discarding coarse spinach stems as they also are particularly good in soups and sauces.
• **Delicate greens:** If your lettuce is no longer fresh and crisp, it can be pureed to a smooth, creamy velouté or ground with herbs, nuts such as walnuts, hazelnuts, or almonds, and a drizzle of olive oil, to make pesto.
• **Roots and tubers:** If you buy organic root vegetables and tubers, wash and scrub them thoroughly and either leave their skins on, or cut away the peel and reserve it for another dish. Jerusalem artichoke and potato peelings make beautifully crisp chips and parsnip peelings add a wonderful flavor to a stock or soup. After thorough washing and blanching, the tops of carrots, radishes, turnips, and beets can be used in pestos, soups, and other dishes.
• **Pods:** Many legume pods are completely edible, particularly if they are harvested when young and tender. Crisp English garden (snap) pea pods can be added to a stock, simmered for a couple of minutes, and then blended and strained for a tasty soup. Fried fava beans pods are another treat.
• **Gourds:** Although winter squashes such as butternuts and pumpkins are traditionally peeled, the skin is edible and can be left on, as long as the squash has not been waxed or treated. The skin of a newly harvested squash is best for eating, as that of older vegetables may be tough. The seeds can be toasted and served with an aperitif or sprinkled over salads.
• **Cruciferous vegetables:** Tough or slightly damaged outer leaves are excellent in soups or stocks and the fibrous ribs from cauliflower leaves can be peeled and sautéed or fried. The peeled stalks of broccoli, romanesco, and cauliflower can be diced and sautéed or eaten raw in salads.
• **Stocks:** These welcome all kinds of trimmings, as long as they are organic, including the tough ends of asparagus stalks, which are too valuable to waste.
Finally, any vegetable trimmings you cannot use can be composted.

Storing fresh vegetables

All vegetables are made up of living cells and must be stored properly to keep them fresh for as long as possible. Different vegetables require different storage conditions but, while refrigeration keeps many fresher for longer, not all need to be chilled. Some keep best away from light, while others dislike changes in temperature. The crisper drawer in the refrigerator, on the high-humidity setting, is the best place for vegetables that wilt or lose moisture easily. The low-humidity setting is best for ethylene-producing vegetables, such as avocados. Clean the vegetable drawer frequently to eliminate microbes that could cause spoilage. As soon as vegetables are cut, they begin to discolor and lose nutrients, so store them in an airtight container in the refrigerator and use within 24 hours.

Fruits (tomatoes, zucchini, avocados, bell peppers, eggplants, etc.)

Zucchini, bell peppers, and eggplants are sold when they are already ripe and should be stored in the crisper drawer of the refrigerator. In contrast, tomatoes are a climacteric fruit, meaning they continue to ripen after they have been picked. Storing tomatoes in the refrigerator can mask their flavor and make them taste bland, so it is best to keep them at room temperature. To make tomatoes more refreshing, you can chill them for an hour or two before serving without harming their texture or flavor. Avocados are another climacteric fruit. If already ripe, they can be kept fresh for several days in the refrigerator. Otherwise, store at room temperature until ready to eat. To speed up the ripening process, place an avocado in a paper bag with a high ethylene-producing fruit like a banana or apple. You can use this trick to ripen other climacteric fruits, too.

Leaves (spinach, endives, chard, sorrel, watercress, lettuces, etc.)

Leafy vegetables, especially delicate salad greens, are particularly fragile and should be stored in the crisper drawer in the refrigerator and eaten soon after they are harvested. Hearty greens like chard will last a bit longer—up to four days in the crisper drawer. Pre-packaged salad leaves, which have been packed in a modified atmosphere, should also be kept in the refrigerator, but there is no need to put them in the crisper drawer before the bag is opened.

Stems and bulbs (asparagus, fennel, leeks, celery, garlic, onions, etc.)

The best way to keep asparagus is to wrap the bundle of stalks in a damp dish cloth and place it in the crisper drawer. Celery, fennel, and leeks are a bit hardier and will keep well for five to seven days in the refrigerator. Dried bulb vegetables such as garlic, onions, and shallots should be stored in a cool, dry place away from direct light, but all spring versions—such as green garlic, scallions, and spring onions—should be kept in the refrigerator.

Roots and tubers (potatoes, carrots, celery root, Jerusalem artichokes, Chinese artichokes, radishes, turnips, salsify, rutabaga, etc.)

Long appreciated for their storage potential, most root vegetables and tubers will last for months in a cool, dark place with good ventilation, such as a root cellar or basement. Certain roots and tubers, such as pink radishes and Chinese artichokes, are particularly susceptible to drying out, so should be kept in the refrigerator, as should early varieties such as new potatoes and baby carrots.

Gourds, or cucurbits (pumpkins, summer and winter squash, cucumbers, etc.)

It is not necessary to refrigerate winter squash, such as pumpkins, as they will happily store all winter on a rack in a dry, airy place. However, take care not to knock or damage them as, once bruised, they can quickly develop mold. The flavor of stored winter squash often improves over time as the sugars in them become concentrated. Once cut open, however, winter squash need to be stored in the refrigerator and eaten within a couple of days. Chayotes and thin-skinned summer squash like zucchini will last for up to five days in the refrigerator, ideally in the crisper drawer. Cucumbers are particularly sensitive to cold so keep them in a cool place or, if in the refrigerator, put them in the crisper drawer.

Cruciferous vegetables (cauliflowers, broccoli, cabbages, etc.)

The cabbage family has both fragile members (bok choy, arugula, cauliflower) that need to be refrigerated and eaten quickly and hardier varieties (cabbage) that will keep for longer when chilled. Like the gourds, cabbage family members do not like rough treament, so transport and handle them carefully.

Legumes, or pods (fava beans, peas, and other beans)

Fava beans, peas, and other shelling beans in the legume family do not keep for long unless they are dried (that is to say, mature). The fresh versions are actually immature legumes, which is why they are so delicate. Fresh, they will keep for three days in the refrigerator.

Mushrooms

Mushrooms are fragile. They prefer to be kept in the dark and thrive in humid environments that prevent them from drying out. Mushrooms will sweat and become slimy if stored in plastic bags, so keep them in paper bags which will allow air to circulate while still retaining moisture. Store mushrooms in the crisper drawer of the refrigerator or a cool cellar, away from any strong-smelling foods, as they quickly absorb odors.

Other ways to preserve vegetables

• **Fermentation:** used for sauerkraut or kimchi, as well as other vegetables made into certain pickles.

• **Pickling:** used for vegetables such as cucumbers, radishes, beans, or onions, preserved in a brine solution or acid (vinegar or lemon juice).

• **Drying:** a method that has long been used in warm climates to preserve a wide range of vegetables, including tomatoes, zucchini, bell peppers, and eggplants. It is also an excellent way of preserving mushrooms and retaining their flavor.

• **Canning:** involves heating vegetables to between 230°F–250°F (110°C–120°C) to kill harmful microbes and then sealing them in an airtight steel container. The intensive heat treatment can result in vegetables losing color, flavor, nutrients, and texture.

• **Freezing (0°F/–18°C):** to ensure minimal damage to fibers and to destroy microorganisms that can cause spoilage, first blanch vegetables in boiling salted water, cool them quickly, and then freeze in airtight containers or bags.

Vegetable Seasons around the World

This table provides general guidelines as to the standard harvesting seasons of the vegetables listed. However, the exact range depends on the latitude and climate where you live, as well as other factors. Although many vegetables are available fresh year-round in supermarkets, outside their local cultivation season they are likely to have been grown in greenhouses or transported from other parts of the world. Those harvested at peak ripeness and sold close to where they are grown yield superior nutrients and flavor. Whenever possible, let local farmers' markets be your guide.

SPRING

- Artichoke, globe
- Artichoke, Jerusalem (sunchoke)
- Asparagus
- Avocado
- Beans, fava (broad)
- Beans, green
- Beet (beetroot)
- Bell pepper (capsicum)
- Bok choy (pak choi)
- Broccoli
- Brussels sprouts
- Cabbage, green
- Cabbage, Napa (Chinese leaf)
- Cabbage, red
- Cabbage, white
- Carrot
- Cauliflower
- Cauliflower, romanesco
- Celery
- Celery root (celeriac)
- Corn
- Crosne (Chinese artichoke)
- Cucumber
- Curly endive & escarole
- Eggplant (aubergine)
- Endive (chicory)
- Fennel
- Garlic
- Kale
- Leeks
- Lettuces
- Lettuce, Batavian
- Lettuce, lamb's (mâche, corn salad)
- Mushrooms, button
- Onion
- Parsnip
- Peas
- Potato
- Radish
- Radish, black
- Radish, red
- Rutabaga (swede)
- Scorzonera (salsify)
- Shallots
- Sorrel
- Spinach
- Squash, summer
- Squash, winter
- Sugar snap peas (mangetouts)
- Swiss chard
- Turnip
- Watercress
- Zucchini (courgette)

SUMMER

- Artichoke, globe
- Asparagus
- Avocado
- Beans, fava (broad)
- Beans, green
- Beet (beetroot)
- Bell pepper (capsicum)
- Bok choy (pak choi)
- Brussels sprouts
- Cabbage, green
- Cabbage, Napa (Chinese leaf)
- Cabbage, red
- Cabbage, white
- Carrot
- Celery
- Corn
- Cucumber
- Curly endive & escarole
- Eggplant (aubergine)
- Endive (chicory)
- Fennel
- Garlic
- Leeks
- Lettuces
- Lettuce, Batavian
- Mushrooms, button
- Onion
- Peas
- Potato
- Potato, Vitelotte
- Radish
- Radish, black
- Radish, red
- Shallots
- Sorrel
- Spinach
- Squash, summer
- Sugar snap peas (mangetouts)
- Swiss chard
- Watercress
- Zucchini (courgette)

FALL

- Artichoke, globe
- Artichoke, Jerusalem (sunchoke)
- Avocado
- Beans, green
- Beet (beetroot)
- Bell pepper (capsicum)
- Bok choy (pak choi)
- Broccoli
- Brussels sprouts
- Cabbage, green
- Cabbage, Napa (Chinese leaf)
- Cabbage, red
- Cabbage, white
- Carrot
- Cauliflower
- Cauliflower, romanesco
- Celery
- Celery root (celeriac)
- Chayote
- Corn
- Crosne (Chinese artichoke)
- Curly endive & escarole
- Cucumber
- Eggplant (aubergine)
- Endive (chicory)
- Fennel
- Garlic
- Kale
- Lettuces
- Lettuce, Batavian
- Lettuce, lamb's (mâche, corn salad)
- Mushrooms, button
- Onion
- Parsnip
- Peas
- Potato
- Potato, Vitelotte
- Pumpkin
- Radish
- Radish, black
- Radish, red
- Rutabaga (swede)
- Scorzonera (salsify)
- Shallots
- Spinach
- Squash, summer
- Squash, winter
- Sweet potato
- Swiss chard
- Turnip
- Watercress
- Zucchini (courgette)

WINTER

- Artichoke, Jerusalem (sunchoke)
- Avocado
- Beans, fava (broad)
- Beet (beetroot)
- Bell pepper (capsicum)
- Bok choy (pak choi)
- Broccoli
- Brussels sprouts
- Cabbage, green
- Cabbage, Napa (Chinese leaf)
- Cabbage, red
- Cabbage, white
- Carrot
- Cauliflower
- Cauliflower, romanesco
- Celery
- Celery root (celeriac)
- Chayote
- Crosne (Chinese artichoke)
- Eggplant (aubergine)
- Endive (chicory)
- Fennel
- Garlic
- Kale
- Leeks
- Lettuces
- Lettuce, Batavian
- Lettuce, lamb's (mâche, corn salad)
- Mushrooms, button
- Onion
- Parsnip
- Peas
- Potato
- Pumpkin
- Radish, daikon
- Rutabaga (swede)
- Scorzonera (salsify)
- Spinach
- Squash, winter
- Sweet potato
- Swiss chard
- Turnip
- Watercress

EQUIPMENT

UTENSILS

1. Tomato peeler
2. Vegetable peeler
3. Curved bird's beak turning knife
4. Paring knife
5. Filleting knife
6. Chopping or chef's knife

1. 4-sided box grater and flat grater
2. China cap or conical strainer
3. Fine-mesh sieve or strainer
4. Mandoline + combs
5. Melon ballers
6. Zester with a channel knife
7. Razor peeler or swivel vegetable peeler
8. Whisk
9. Skimmer

1. Saucepan and pot lids
2. Steamer
3. Small, medium, and large saucepans
4. Deep-frying pan + basket
5. Vegetable mill + grinding disks

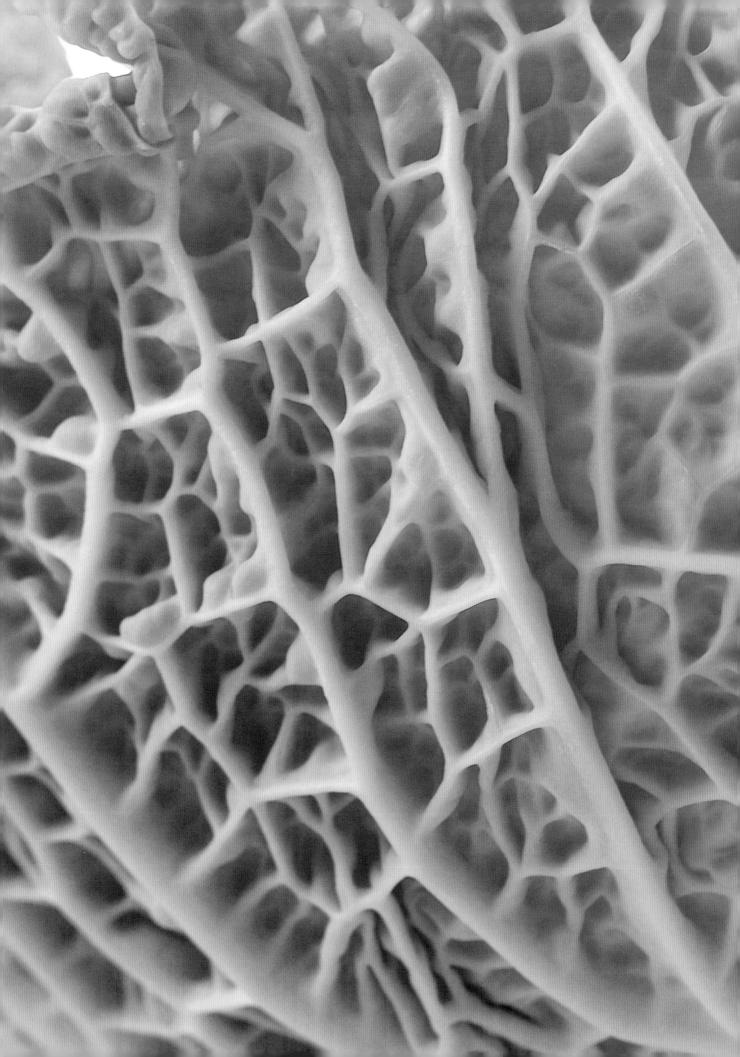

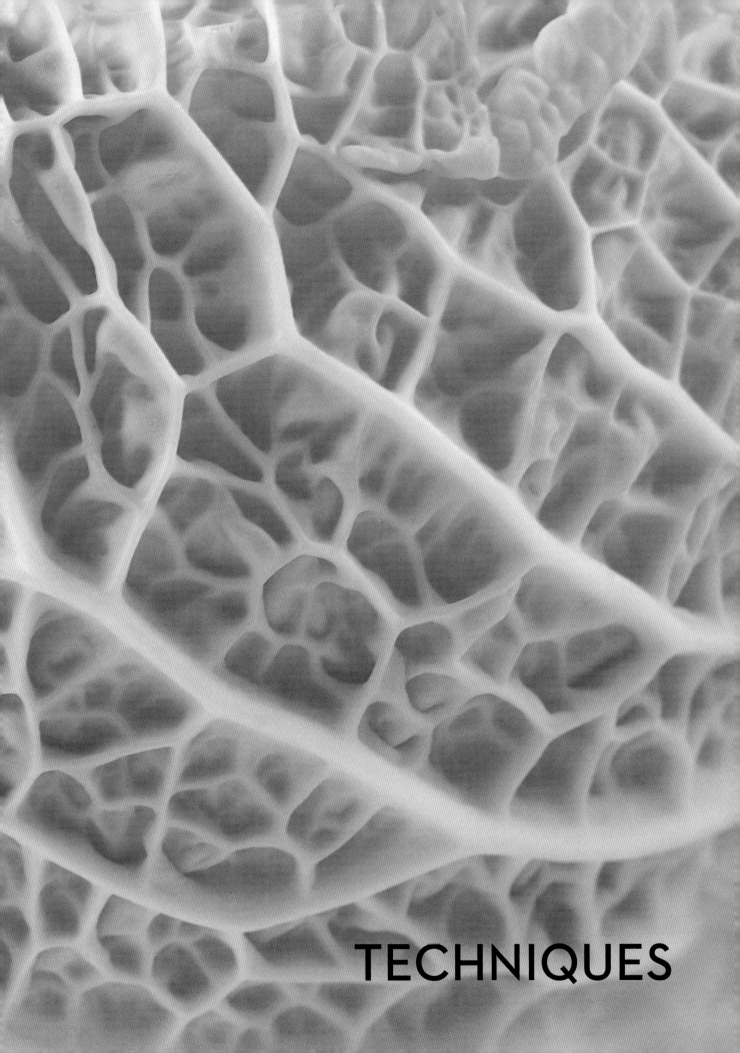

TECHNIQUES

PREPARATION
AND CLEANING

Washing Lettuce

Washing salad leaves (romaine/cos lettuce, batavia, frisée, oak leaf lettuce, lamb's lettuce, arugula) individually in a bowl of cold water with a little vinegar added ensures any impurities such as dirt, grit, or aphids are removed, as well as any damaged leaves.

Ingredients
Distilled white vinegar
(⅓ cup/80 ml
to 4 cups/1 liter water)

Lettuce

Equipment
Chef's knife

Lettuce spinner

1 • Fill a large bowl to three-quarters with cold water and add the vinegar.

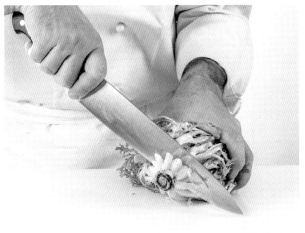

2 • Cut off the base of the lettuce.

3 • Carefully pull off the lettuce leaves one at a time and immerse them in the water.

4 • Lift the leaves out of the water with your hands.

5 • Place the leaves in a salad spinner and spin until dry.

Washing and Storing Herbs

Ingredients

Distilled white vinegar (⅓ cup/80 ml
to 4 cups/1 liter water)

Fresh herbs

CHEFS' NOTES

Once the herbs are well wrapped,
they can be kept in an airtight container
in the refrigerator for several days.

1 • Put the water and vinegar in a large bowl
and immerse the herbs in it.

2 • Dampen a few sheets of paper towel,
remove the herbs from the water,
and place them on the paper towel.

3 • Roll the paper towel around the herbs.

4 • Be careful not to roll them too tightly.
Refrigerate until needed.

Cleaning Leeks or Fennel Bulbs

Ingredients
Leeks
Fennel bulbs
Distilled white vinegar
(⅓ cup/80 ml to 4 cups/1 liter
water)

Equipment
Chef's knife

CHEFS' NOTES

Choose leeks that have a large white part
and a bright green top.

1 • Cut off about two-thirds of the green part of the
leeks and slit the leeks in half lengthwise.

2 • Trim off the small roots at the base.
Remove the damaged outer leaves.

3 • Cut fennel bulbs in half lengthwise and then make
a triangular cut to remove the tough cores.

Cleaning Leeks or Fennel Bulbs (continued)

4 • Remove the damaged outer leaves.

5 • Add the vinegar to a bowl of cold water and wash the leeks thoroughly to remove all the dirt between the layers.

6 • Remove the leeks from the water.

7 • Wash the fennel in the same way in a bowl of clean cold water with vinegar added, rinsing thoroughly between the layers.

Cleaning Mushrooms

Ingredients

Mushrooms

Equipment

Paring knife

Soft pastry brush or
mushroom brush

1 • If the mushrooms are large (for example, porcini), cut the stems
to a point.

Cleaning Mushrooms (continued)

2 • For smaller mushrooms, cut off the earthy base.

3 • Immerse mushrooms such as chanterelles or black trumpets in cold water and briefly swirl them around, before lifting them out of the water.

4 • Use a damp brush to clean hedgehog or sweet tooth (*pied de mouton*) or porcini mushrooms. Avoid immersing them in water as they risk absorbing too much liquid.

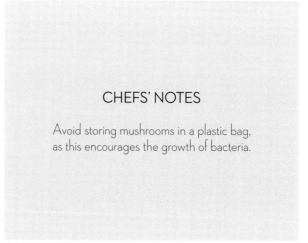

CHEFS' NOTES

Avoid storing mushrooms in a plastic bag, as this encourages the growth of bacteria.

Preparing Asparagus

Ingredients
Asparagus

Equipment
Paring knife
Razor-type vegetable peeler
Kitchen twine

CHEFS' NOTES

Choose straight, firm asparagus stalks that have buds with tight scales and a slightly shiny base.

1 • Trim the base of each asparagus stalk, as they are often woody or damaged, and remove the small scales along the stem with a paring knife.

2 • Holding each stalk flat, carefully peel the asparagus stem with a razor peeler.

3 • Using the tip of a knife, lightly score each stalk to mark the base of the tip.

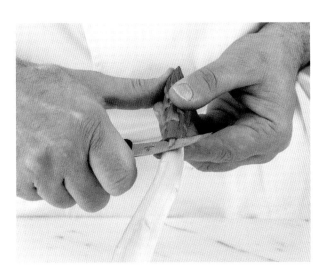

4 • Peel the stalks up to the scored mark.

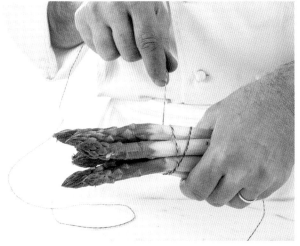

5 • Tie into bundles of about 8 asparagus stalks, depending on how thick they are, wrapping the twine around them 2 or 3 times to hold them in place.

6 • Tie the twine in a knot so the stalks stay firmly in place.

Peeling and Seeding Tomatoes

This technique can also be used to peel fava beans, raw almonds, peaches, and nectarines.

Ingredients
Tomatoes

Equipment
Paring knife
Skimmer

1 • Using the tip of a paring knife, cut out the tomato stalks.

2 • Cut a cross in the base of each tomato.

3 • Lower the tomatoes into a saucepan of boiling water and leave for 20 seconds.

Peeling and Seeding Tomatoes (continued)

4 • Lift the tomatoes out with a skimmer and immediately immerse them in a bowl of cold water to prevent them cooking further.

5 • Peel off the skin, which will come away easily.

6 • Cut the tomatoes in half lengthwise.

7 • Carefully scoop out the seeds using a spoon, leaving just the flesh.

Peeling and Seeding Bell Peppers
OVEN METHOD

Ingredients

Bell peppers
Olive oil

Cooking time

40 minutes

Equipment

Roasting pan with
grill rack

Paring knife

1 • Preheat the oven to 275°F (140°C/Gas mark 1).
Place the bell peppers on a grill rack and drizzle or brush with oil.
Roast in the oven for 40 minutes.

Peeling and Seeding Bell Peppers
OVEN METHOD (continued)

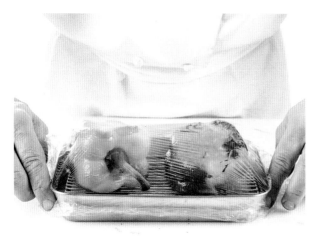

2 • When the peppers are cooked, cover them with plastic wrap, and let cool.

3 • Using a paring knife, peel away the skins of the peppers.

4 • Pull off the stems, cut the peppers in half, and remove the ribs with the seeds attached.

CHEFS' NOTES

The peeled peppers can be kept in a sealed jar, immersed in olive oil with garlic and thyme sprigs, for 5–7 days in the refrigerator.

Peeling Bell Peppers
KITCHEN TORCH METHOD

Ingredients
Bell peppers

Equipment
Kitchen torch

Resting time
20 minutes

1• Using a kitchen torch, char the pepper skins on all sides, holding each pepper by its stem and taking great care not to burn yourself.

2 • When the skin is blackened all over, cover with plastic wrap and let rest for about 20 minutes.

3 • Remove the plastic wrap and immerse the peppers in a bowl of cold water to make it easier to pull away the skins. Peel the peppers so no small pieces of skin remain attached.

CHEFS' NOTES

You can also char the pepper skins on the flame of a gas stove top or over a barbecue, protecting your hand by wearing an oven mitt, skewering the pepper on a toasting fork, or holding it with barbecue tongs.

Shelling Peas

Ingredients

Garden peas

Open each pod by pressing it lightly along the seam.
When the pod pops, open it and push out the peas using your fingers.

Preparing Green Beans

Ingredients
Green beans

1 • Using your thumb and index finger, snap off the end of each bean where it joins the stem.

CHEFS' NOTES

Choose beans that are firm, regular in shape, and a vivid green color.

2 • If there is a string running down the seam, remove this by pulling it away. Snap off the other end in the same way.

Preparing a Vegetable Puree

Ingredients

Vegetables such as carrots, turnips, or potatoes

1 garlic clove

Butter

Salt and freshly ground pepper

Equipment

Chef's knife

Food mill

1 • Wash and peel the vegetables. Cut them into even-sized pieces.

CHEFS' NOTES

You can give your purees an extra zing by adding a drizzle of a flavored oil, such as nut oil, sesame oil, or even chili oil, mixing it in at the end.

2 • Peel the garlic and using the flat part of the knife blade, press down hard on the clove to crush it.

3 • Cook the vegetables and garlic in a saucepan of boiling salted water until very tender.

4 • Drain in a colander over a bowl, reserving the cooking liquid to be used as stock for other recipes.

5 • While still warm, pass the vegetables through a food mill, turning the handle to crush them to a puree.

6 • Using a flexible spatula, mix in a small knob of butter to make the puree smoother. Season as necessary with salt and pepper.

CUTTING AND CHOPPING

Chopping Herbs

Ingredients
Fresh herbs, leaves picked, washed, and dried

Equipment
Chef's knife

CHEFS' NOTES

• This technique should not be used for chives, as if the blade is moved backwards and forwards, the stems will be bruised and will oxidize and blacken. Make single cuts with the blade across the stems, or snip them using scissors.

• Chop and add delicate herbs, such as parsley, basil, and cilantro, to hot dishes just before serving to preserve their flavor.

1 • Shape the herb leaves into a mound with your fingers and roughly chop the leaves.

2 • Position the knife parallel to you. Hold down the tip of the blade with one hand and lift the heel with the other.

3 • Making rocking motions with the knife, cut across the herbs until they are finely chopped.

Slicing Onions

Ingredients
Onions

Equipment
Chef's knife

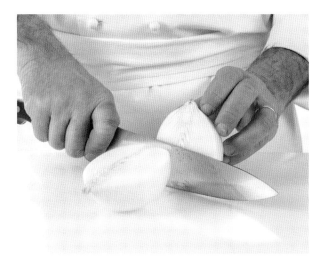

1 • Peel the onions and cut them in half lengthwise.

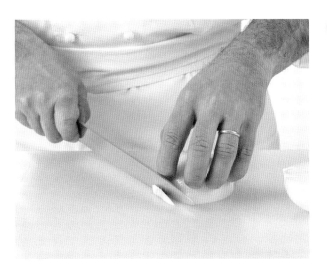

2 • Place cut side down and trim off the base.

3 • Cut each half into thin slices about ⅛ in. (2–3 mm) thick.

Chopping Shallots

Ingredients
Shallots

Equipment
Paring knife

1 • Peel the shallots and cut them in half lengthwise.

CHEFS' NOTES

You can also chop fresh herbs by rolling them up into tight bundles and chopping them as finely or as coarsely as you require.

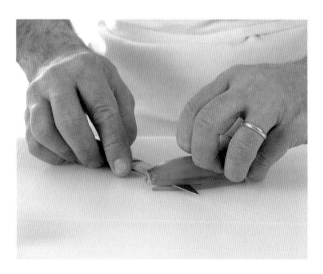

2 • Place cut side down and hold the base with your fingers bent under. With the knife parallel to the cutting board, make several horizontal cuts from the tip of the shallot, stopping just short of the base.

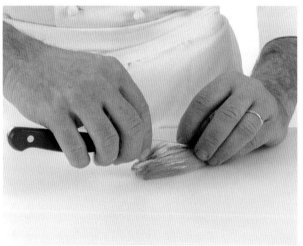

3 • Continue by making several vertical cuts lengthwise.

4 • Make crosswise cuts close together,
parallel to your fingers, to chop finely.

Julienne Cut

Julienned vegetables feature in many French dishes, such as potage julienne Darblay,
a potato soup with finely cut strips of different colored vegetables. This technique can be used
to cut a large variety of vegetables.

Ingredients
Carrots
Leeks

Equipment
Mandoline
Chef's knife

1 • Wash and peel the carrots.
   Cut them into 2-in. (5-cm) lengths and slice
   using a mandoline.

2 • Cut the slices into very fine strips.

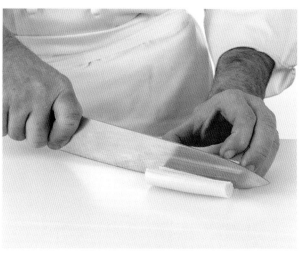

3 • Wash the leeks, cut the white part only into 2-in.
   (5-cm) lengths, and then cut in half lengthwise.

4 • Cut into very thin strips.

Brunoise Cut

This specific technique for cutting vegetables into evenly sized ¹⁄₁₆-in. (2-mm) dice is used for making hand-cut vegetable soups, such as minestrone and potage cultivateur ("farmers' soup"), aromatic garnishes, and stuffings for poultry or fish.

Ingredients
Carrots or other firm vegetables

Equipment
Chef's knife
Mandoline

1 • Wash and peel the carrots. Cut them lengthwise into pieces, trimming the ends and sides flat. Cut into thin slices using a mandoline.

2 • Cut the slices into sticks about ¹⁄₁₆ in. (2 mm) wide.

3 • Cut the sticks into ¹⁄₁₆-in. (2-mm) cubes.

Paysanne Cut

This is a simple way to slice vegetables such as carrots, leeks, celery, and turnips and leaves few trimmings.

Ingredients
Carrots

Equipment
Chef's knife

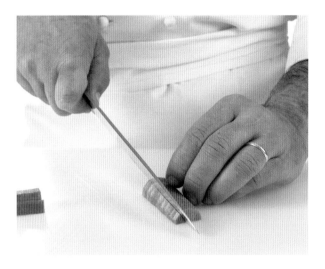

1 • Wash and peel the carrots. Cut them in half lengthwise and then cut each half into three.

CHEFS' NOTES

You can also use this cut
to make squares of just under ½ in. (1 cm),
1⁄16 in. (2 mm) thick, for soups.

2 • Finely chop each half into pieces about 1⁄16 in. (2 mm) thick.

Mirepoix Cut

A mirepoix is a mix of different vegetables, such as carrots, onions, and celery, cut into large dice and used for making stocks, sauces, and aromatic garnishes.

Ingredients
Onions
Carrots

Equipment
Chef's knife

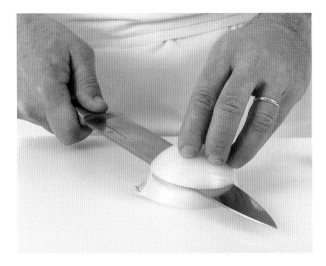

1 • Peel and cut the onions in half lengthwise. With the knife blade parallel to the cutting board, make 1 or 2 horizontal incisions (depending on the size of the onion), stopping just short of the base.

2 • Slice vertically 3 or 4 times (depending on the size of the onion) to make large, evenly sized cubes.

3 • Wash and peel the carrots. Trim the top and base of each and cut in half lengthwise. Cut each piece in half again.

4 • Holding the two pieces of each half together,
cut across into large, evenly sized cubes.

Cutting Angled Slices

*This is a practical way to cut cylindrical shaped vegetables
such as leeks, carrots, cucumbers, and courgettes.*

Ingredients

Leeks, or other
cylindrical shaped
vegetables

Equipment

Chef's knife

Wash the vegetables. Holding the vegetable with the fingers of one
hand bent under, use the knife in the other hand to cut into angled
slices of the same thickness.

Macedoine Cut

This is a technique for cutting vegetables and fruits into dice that are between the size of brunoise and mirepoix. The vegetables are usually boiled separately à l'anglaise, *then refreshed and drained before being mixed with mayonnaise as a cold starter or with butter as a garnish.*

Ingredients
Carrots
Turnips

Equipment
Chef's knife

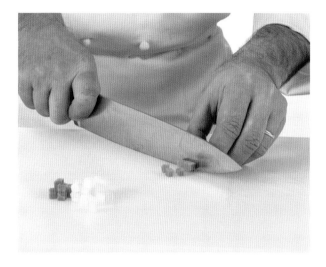

1 • Wash and peel the carrots and turnips. Cut them into sticks about ¼ in. (5 mm) wide.

CHEFS' NOTES

You can use a mandoline
to cut the vegetables into sticks before
cutting them crosswise into macedoine.

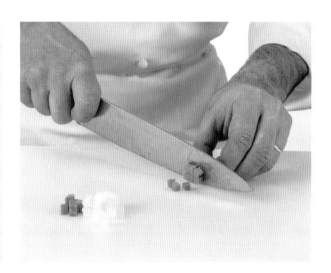

2 • Stack several sticks on top of each other and cut crosswise into ¼-in. (5-mm) dice.

Turning a Globe Artichoke

Ingredients
Globe artichokes
Lemon slices or 1 tsp (5 g) citric acid

Equipment
Paring knife
Melon baller

1 • Snap off the artichoke stem with your hand to break the fibers in the heart.

CHEFS' NOTES

It is important to choose artichokes carefully. Before buying, check they feel heavy, their leaves are closed and tightly packed, and they have no dark spots or other blemishes.

2 • Pull off the outer leaves and most of the smaller, tender leaves.

3 • Using the paring knife, trim the central leaves level with the heart.

Turning a Globe Artichoke (continued)

4 • Trim the artichoke heart.

5 • Cut away the green part on the underside of the artichoke.

6 • Using the melon baller, scrape out the hairy choke.

7 • Trim the edges of the heart to make them smooth.

8 • Reserve the prepared artichoke hearts in a bowl of cold water
with lemon slices or citric acid added to prevent them turning brown,
until ready to use.

Turning a Small Purple Artichoke

Ingredients

Small purple artichokes

1 lemon, or ½ lemon
and 1 tsp (5 g) citric acid

Equipment

Paring knife or curved bird's beak
turning knife

Melon baller

1 • Cut off the artichoke stem about 2 in. (4–5 cm)
below the base.

2 • Pull off the outer leaves and then most
of the softer inner leaves. Trim the central leaves
level with the heart.

3 • Peel the stem.

4 • Trim the artichoke heart.

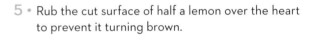

5 • Rub the cut surface of half a lemon over the heart to prevent it turning brown.

6 • Cut in half lengthwise and use the melon baller to scoop out the hairy choke.

7 • Add half a lemon, cut into slices, or the citric acid to a bowl of cold water and reserve the artichokes in the water until ready to use.

Turning a Mushroom

Ingredients
Button mushrooms

Equipment
Paring knife

CHEFS' NOTES

You can also use this technique
on artichoke hearts.

1 • Holding the knife by the blade, position it on top
of a mushroom and press down lightly.

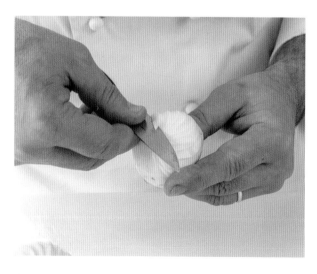

2 • Starting at the center, make incisions at regular
intervals and close together, following the curve
of the cap.

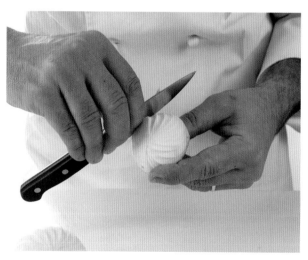

3 • For each incision, tilt the blade diagonally toward
the bottom of the cap.

4 • Repeat this around the entire cap.

Scalloping a Mushroom

Ingredients
Button mushrooms

Equipment
Paring knife

1 • Cut off the mushroom stems. Holding the knife at an angle, cut the caps in half diagonally.

CHEFS' NOTES

Choose button mushrooms carefully:
the cap must be tightly closed around the stem.

2 • Still holding the knife at an angle, cut the caps in half again to make angled quarters.

Preparing Mushroom Duxelles

Ingredients
Button mushrooms

Equipment
Long, thin-bladed knife

1 • Cut off the mushroom stems and then slice the caps horizontally into three.

2 • Holding the knife parallel to you, cut each cap into three or four.

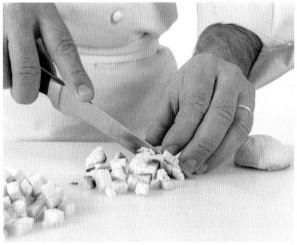

3 • Cut into ⅛-in. (2–3-mm) dice.

Turning a Potato

Ingredients
Potatoes

Equipment
Paring knife or curved bird's beak turning knife

CHEFS' NOTES

• It is important to choose a variety of potato with firm, waxy flesh.

• Cutting potatoes into pieces of the same size and shape ensures they cook evenly when sautéed.

1 • Wash and peel the potatoes and trim the ends. Cut the potatoes into halves or quarters, depending on their size.

2 • Take a piece of potato and, holding it firmly with your thumb, move the knife blade from top to bottom, paring off a little of the outer flesh each time.

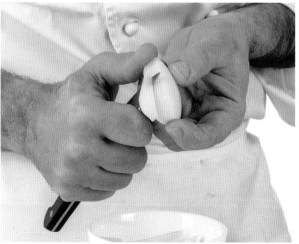

3 • Repeat this, turning the potato regularly until it is an elongated oval shape.

Preparing Parisian Fried Potatoes

Pommes Pont-Neuf

*This name was given to Parisian fried potatoes in the 1830s,
when they were sold on the riverbanks by the Pont-Neuf bridge in Paris.*

Ingredients
Large potatoes

Equipment
Chef's knife

CHEFS' NOTES

It is recommended to cook the potatoes
in two separate oil baths. Precook them by frying
at 320°F (160°C) for 4–6 minutes and then fry them
a second time at 360°F (180°C) for a few minutes,
until they are golden brown. This ensures they are
crisp on the outside and fluffy on the inside.

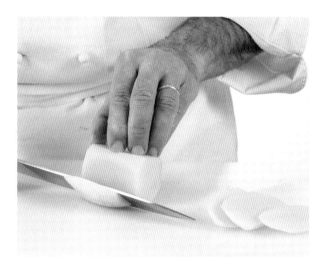

1 • Wash, peel, and trim the potatoes into blocks with straight sides.

2 • Cut into slices about ½ in. (1 cm) thick.

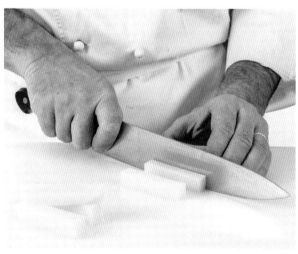

3 • Cut the slices into sticks about ½ in. (1 cm) wide.

Preparing Pommes Anna

Ingredients
Potatoes

Equipment
1½-in. (3.5-cm) round cookie cutter
Mandoline
Pommes Anna pan or non-stick skillet

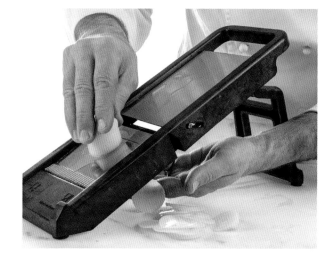

1 • Wash and peel the potatoes. Using the cookie cutter, trim the potatoes into equal-sized cylinders. Cut the cylinders into slices about ¹⁄₁₆ in. (2 mm) thick, using a mandoline.

2 • To assemble, place one potato slice in the center of the pan and then overlap the remaining slices in neat concentric circles around it.

3 • Make sure the slices are evenly spaced apart and continue to build up the layers until the pan has been filled.

Preparing Potato Wafers

Ingredients
Potatoes

Equipment
Mandoline with a rippled blade

1 • Wash and peel the potatoes. Using the mandoline fitted with a rippled blade, slice the potatoes about 1/16 in. (2 mm) thick.

CHEFS' NOTES

• After slicing the potatoes, it is very important to rinse them thoroughly in clean, cold water to remove excess starch. Drain and dry them thoroughly, taking care not to damage them, and then deep-fry in small batches in hot oil at 340°F (170°C).

• You can also prepare sweet potatoes or vitelottes (a variety of French potato that is deep purple in color) in the same way.

2 • Each time you cut a slice, rotate the potato one quarter-turn to create a pattern of small holes.

Preparing Matchstick Potatoes

Ingredients
Potatoes

Equipment
Mandoline
Chef's knife

1 • Wash and peel the potatoes. Using the mandoline, cut the potatoes into slices about ¼ in. (5 mm) thick.

CHEFS' NOTES

Choose floury potatoes such as Bintje, Russet Burbank, Agria, or Maris Piper, as their high starch content ensures a crisper, lighter result.

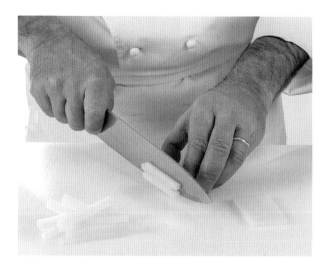

2 • Trim the edges of the slices so they are straight, then cut into sticks about ¼ in. (5 mm) wide.

Preparing Vegetable Tagliatelle

Ingredients
Black radishes, or other vegetables such as
zucchini, carrots, sweet potatoes

Equipment
Mandoline
Chef's knife

1 • Wash and peel the vegetables.
Using the mandoline, cut them lengthwise
into thin slices about 1/16 in. (1 mm) thick.

CHEFS' NOTES

To cook the vegetable tagliatelle,
blanch it quickly to ensure it remains al dente,
toss it in a skillet with melted butter, and season
with herbs or spices of your choice.

2 • Stack several slices on top of one another
and then cut into strips about 1/2 in. (1 cm) wide.

Cutting Grooved Vegetable Slices

Ingredients
Carrots

Equipment
Zester with a channel knife
Chef's knife

CHEFS' NOTES

Grooved carrot slices are often added
to broths or stocks as an aromatic garnish.

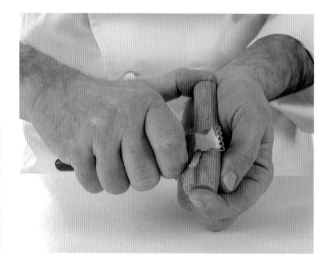

1 • Wash and peel the carrots. Run the ridged channel
knife on a zester tool down a carrot from top
to bottom, pressing firmly to cut a groove.

2 • Repeat at regular intervals around the carrot.

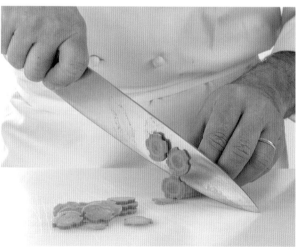

3 • Cut the carrot crosswise into grooved slices.

Preparing Vegetable Balls

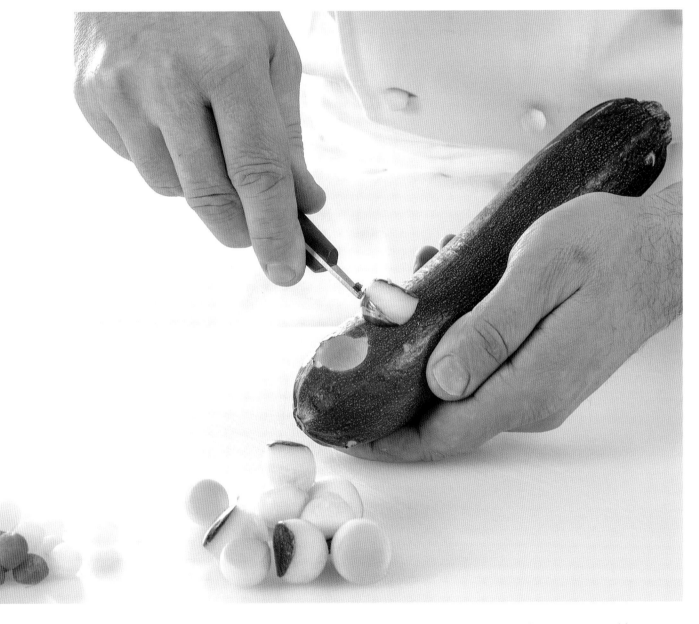

Ingredients

Vegetables such as zucchini, carrots, and turnips

Equipment

Melon baller

Wash the vegetables. Press the melon baller into a vegetable and twist to extract a small ball of the flesh.

COOKING

Blanching Cabbage

This technique is used to precook and soften cabbage leaves before use.

Ingredients
Cabbage
Salt

Cooking time
3–4 minutes

Equipment
Skimmer
Wire rack for drying

1 • Peel the leaves off the cabbage. Fill a bowl with cold water and ice cubes. Add the leaves (in batches, if necessary) to a large saucepan of well-salted boiling water.

2 • Bring the water back to a boil and keep the leaves submerged by pressing down on them with a skimmer. Cook for 3–4 minutes.

3 • Lift the leaves out of the water using the skimmer, and refresh in the bowl of ice water. Drain on a rack before using.

Parboiling Potatoes

This technique is used to eliminate impurities and precook potatoes before cooking them in another way, such as sautéing.

Ingredients
Potatoes

Equipment
Skimmer

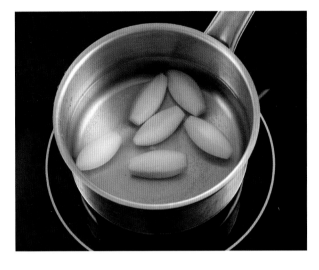

1 • Wash, peel, and, if you wish, turn the potatoes (see technique p. 78). Put them in a saucepan of cold water.

CHEFS' NOTES

• Use this technique, which cuts down on cooking time, before sautéing, roasting, grilling, or deep-frying potatoes.

• Parboiling differs from blanching in that the vegetables are not immersed in ice water immediately after removing them from the boiling water.

2 • Bring to a boil, cook for a few minutes, and then drain the potatoes by lifting them out using a skimmer.

Boiling à *l'Anglaise*

Ingredients

Green beans (or other green vegetables, prepared as necessary)

Salt

Cooking time

About 5 minutes

Equipment

Skimmer

1 • Wash and trim the green beans (see technique p. 49). Add them to a large saucepan of boiling salted water and let boil for 4–5 minutes, depending on how thick they are.

CHEFS' NOTES

This quick-cooking method preserves all the flavor of a vegetable, as well as its vitamins.

2 • Fill a bowl with water and ice cubes. When the beans are cooked *al dente*, drain them using a skimmer.

3 • Immediately plunge the beans into the ice water for a few seconds, to prevent them cooking further and to retain their bright green color (from the chlorophyll pigment they contain).

Steaming

This is a cooking method by steam, without using fat and with no direct contact with water.

Ingredients
Vegetables

Equipment
Steamer

1 • Wash, peel, and cut the vegetables into smaller pieces or leave whole, as necessary.

2 • Fill the lower part of a steamer with water and place the vegetables in the upper part.

3 • Cover and cook until the vegetables are tender all the way through.

Poaching

This technique concentrates taste and color, and limits exchanges with the cooking liquid.

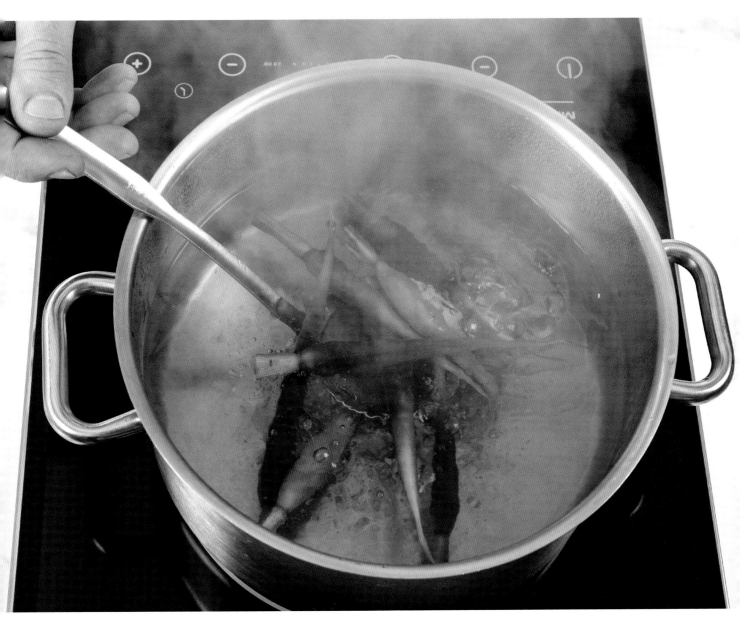

Ingredients
Carrots
Salt

Equipment
Skimmer

Add the carrots to a large pan of boiling salted water. Cook until tender and then lift out using a skimmer.

Braising

This technique consists of slowly cooking certain vegetables, such as lettuces, endives (chicory), fennel bulbs, or turnips, in a covered pan in the oven on a bed of aromatic vegetables and herbs with a little water or vegetable stock.

Ingredients

Full-flavored vegetables and herbs such as onions, carrots, garlic cloves, thyme sprigs

Butter

Little gem or other lettuce

Vegetable stock

Cooking time

30 minutes

1 • Wash and peel the vegetables. Cut the onions and carrots paysanne-style (see technique p. 61). Sauté them in a little butter in an ovenproof saucepan, without coloring them.

2 • Add the lettuce, and then the garlic and thyme.

3 • Pour in enough vegetable stock to cover the vegetables.

4 • Cut a disk of parchment paper the same diameter as the saucepan. Make a hole in the center of the disk and place it on top of the vegetables.

5 • Bring to a boil, then cover with a lid and place in a 350°F (180°C/Gas mark 4) oven for about 30 minutes.

CHEFS' NOTES

Instead of parchment paper, you can cover the vegetables with a layer of pork rind. It will prevent the vegetables from drying out in the oven and also add extra flavor to the stock.

Grilling

Ingredients

Zucchini (or other vegetables such as bell peppers or eggplant)

Olive oil

Salt and freshly ground pepper

Equipment

Cast iron ridged grill pan

Mandoline

1 • Heat the grill pan until very hot. Pour in a little oil and, using a thick pad of paper towel, smear it evenly over the pan. While the grill pan is heating, wash and cut the zucchini into thin slices lengthwise, using a mandoline.

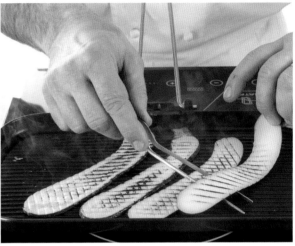

2 • Season the slices with salt and pepper and place on the hot grill. Drizzle with a little more oil, brushing it over the slices to coat them evenly.

3 • Turn the slices over. You can arrange them at different angles so the scorch lines from the grill pan ridges create attractive patterns.

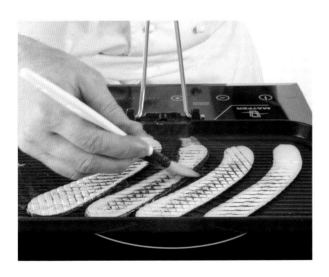

4 • Brush the slices again with oil.

5 • Lift them out and transfer to a serving platter.

Deep-Frying Onions

Ingredients

Onions
Whole or reduced-fat milk
All-purpose flour
Oil for deep-frying
Salt and freshly ground pepper

Equipment

Large pot with deep-frying basket
or deep fryer
Skimmer

1 • Peel the onions, slice them into thin rounds,
and separate into rings. Dip briefly in milk
and then roll in flour until evenly coated.
Heat the oil to 355°F (180°C). Carefully add
the rings to the very hot oil.

2 • Let the rings deep-fry, working in batches,
if necessary; if too many onions are added at once,
they will lower the temperature of the oil.

3 • When the rings are golden brown, lift them out
using the skimmer.

4 • Place on a tray or large plate lined with paper towel to drain off excess oil. Season with salt and pepper.

Deep-Frying in a Bread-crumb Coating

Ingredients

Potatoes (or other vegetables)

Flour

Beaten egg

Fine bread crumbs

Oil for deep-frying

Equipment

Large pot with deep-frying basket or deep fryer

Skimmer

1 • Wash and peel the potatoes. Cut them into fairly thick slices and roll them in flour until well coated.

2 • Coat the floured slices in beaten egg.

3 • Finally, roll them in the bread crumbs to cover them on all sides.

4 • Heat the oil to 355°F (180°C) Carefully add the slices to the hot oil and deep-fry them until the bread-crumb coating is golden brown.

5 • Lift out using the skimmer and drain on a plate lined with paper towel.

Deep-Frying in Tempura Batter

Ingredients

¾ cup + 2 tbsp (200 ml) sparkling water

1 egg yolk

¾ cup + 2 tbsp (4 oz./110 g) all-purpose flour

6 large shiso leaves (or other vegetables such as eggplant, mushrooms, or bell peppers)

⅓ cup + 1 tbsp (2 oz./60 g) cornstarch

Peanut oil

Salt

Equipment

Pastry brush

Large pot with deep-frying basket or deep fryer

Skimmer

1 • To make the tempura batter, mix the sparkling water, egg yolk, and flour together.

2 • Brush a little cornstarch over the shiso leaves using the pastry brush, to absorb any humidity and to help coat the leaves in the tempura batter.

3 • Dip each leaf into the tempura batter.

4 • Heat the oil to 355°F (180°C). Carefully lower the coated leaves into the hot oil (work in batches, if necessary) and deep-fry them for a few minutes, until the coating puffs up well.

5 • Lift out using the skimmer and drain on a plate lined with paper towel. Season with salt.

Preparing Confit Vegetables

Ingredients
Unpeeled garlic cloves
Tomatoes
Unpeeled shallots
Herb sprigs such as thyme and rosemary
Olive oil

Place the garlic, tomatoes, and shallots
in separate saucepans and cover with olive oil.
Add the herbs and simmer until the vegetables
are well cooked and tender.

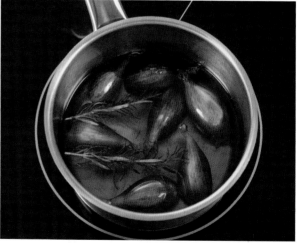

Oven Roasting

Ingredients

Vegetables such as
carrots, potatoes,
pumpkin, onions,
garlic, and shallots,
washed

Herb sprigs
such as thyme
and rosemary

Olive oil

Salt and freshly
ground pepper

Cooking time

30 minutes

Equipment

Non-stick
baking dish

1 • Cut the vegetables in half or into thick slices,
depending on their size. Spread out in a baking dish,
drizzle with olive oil, and tuck herb sprigs among them.

2 • Roast in the oven at 350°F (180°C/Gas mark 4) for
30 minutes, turning the vegetables halfway through,
until tender. Season with salt and pepper.

RECIPES

FRUIT
VEGETABLES

COLD TOMATO AND STRAWBERRY BROTH

Eau de tomate et fraise

Serves 10

Active time
30 minutes

Draining time
Overnight plus
30 minutes

Cooking time
10–30 minutes

Chilling time
30 minutes

Equipment
Blender
Large fine-mesh sieve

Ingredients

Tomato water
5½ lb. (2.5 kg) tomatoes

Strawberry juice
4½ lb. (2 kg)
strawberries
Sugar to taste

To garnish
1 oz. (30 g) tapioca
pearls
20 blanched almonds
10 heirloom tomatoes
in different colors
20 strawberries
Oregano oil
Small chervil sprigs
Small fennel fronds
1 handful fennel flowers

PREPARING THE TOMATO WATER

A day ahead, wash and peel the tomatoes (see technique p. 41) and blend them. Line a large sieve with a clean, damp dish towel and set it over a large mixing bowl. Pour in the blended tomatoes and let drain overnight in the refrigerator.

PREPARING THE STRAWBERRY JUICE

Wash and hull the strawberries. Cut them in half lengthwise, place in a large bowl, sprinkle lightly with sugar to taste, and cover with plastic wrap. Place the bowl over a pan of barely simmering water and let drain for at least 30 minutes. Strain into a bowl, without pressing down too firmly on the strawberries.

PREPARING THE COLD TOMATO AND STRAWBERRY BROTH

Combine the tomato water and strawberry juice according to taste, setting aside some of the strawberry juice. Chill for at least 30 minutes.

PREPARING THE GARNISHES

Cook the Japanese tapioca in a saucepan of boiling water according to the package instructions. Drain, refresh under cold water, and add to the reserved strawberry juice. Cut each almond into 2 or 3 slices lengthwise.

TO SERVE

Peel the heirloom tomatoes (see technique p. 41) and cut into quarters or wedges. Halve or quarter the strawberries. Drizzle enough oregano oil into each serving bowl to cover the base and divide the tomatoes, strawberries, and the rest of the garnishes among them. Pour the tomato and strawberry broth into a jug and add it to each bowl when ready to serve.

TOMATO SALAD, HONEY VINAIGRETTE, AND LOVAGE SORBET

Salade de tomates, vinaigrette au miel, sorbet livèche et huile d'olive

Serves 6

Active time
1 hour

Cooking time
20 minutes

Freezing time
24 hours

Drying time
12 hours

Chilling time
2 hours

Equipment
Ice-cream maker
Immersion blender
Fine-mesh sieve
Siphon + 2 cartridges

Ingredients

Lovage ice cream
1²/₃ cups (400 ml) whole milk
2½ tbsp (1 oz./30 g) sugar
½ tsp (2 g) fleur de sel
¹/₁₀ oz. (3 g) stabilizer (optional)
2 oz. (50 g) lovage leaves
Scant ⅓ cup (70 ml) best-quality olive oil

Black olive soil
6 oz. (180 g) pitted black olives
2 multi-grain crackers, such as Wasa crispbread

Honey vinaigrette
⅔ cup (150 ml) olive oil
⅓ cup (75 ml) grapeseed oil
½ tbsp Savora or Dijon mustard
1½ tbsp (1 oz./30 g) honey

Tomato salad
3 pineapple tomatoes
3 black Krim (black Crimea) tomatoes
3 green zebra tomatoes
3 beefsteak (beef) tomatoes
Fleur de sel
Piment d'Espelette

Mozzarella foam
1 cup (250 ml) whole milk
¾ cup (200 ml) cream, minimum 35% fat
5 oz. (150 g) buffalo mozzarella
Salt and freshly ground pepper

To garnish and serve
A few mizuna leaves
Piment d'Espelette
Fleur de sel

PREPARING THE LOVAGE ICE CREAM

In a heavy saucepan over medium-high heat, bring the milk to a boil with the sugar, fleur de sel, and stabilizer, if using. Let cool, then blend with the lovage. Strain and pour into the bowl of an ice-cream maker. Add the olive oil, incorporate well, and churn according to the manufacturer's instructions. Place in the freezer until serving.

PREPARING THE BLACK OLIVE SOIL

Preheat the oven to 175°F (80°C/Gas at lowest possible setting). Line a baking sheet with parchment paper and spread the olives on it. Dry out in the oven for 12 hours. Let cool, then process to a sandy texture with the crackers, using an immersion blender.

PREPARING THE HONEY VINAIGRETTE

In a mixing bowl, whisk all the ingredients together.

PREPARING THE TOMATO SALAD

Peel the tomatoes (see technique p. 41) and cut them into the shape of your choice. Layer in a dish, pour over the vinaigrette, and season with the fleur de sel and piment d'Espelette. Place in the refrigerator to marinate while you prepare the foam.

PREPARING THE MOZZARELLA FOAM

In a heavy saucepan over medium heat, bring the milk to a boil with the cream. Chop the mozzarella into chunks, add to the saucepan, and stir until melted. Using an immersion blender, process until smooth, season with salt and pepper, and strain. Transfer to a siphon and insert the cartridges. Chill for at least 2 hours before using.

TO SERVE

Make a bed of the black olive soil on each plate and arrange the tomatoes attractively over it. Using the siphon, pipe small amounts of the mozzarella foam between the tomatoes and add a quenelle of lovage ice cream. Garnish with mizuna leaves, dust with piment d'Espelette, and sprinkle over a little fleur de sel.

SAVORY CHEESECAKE WITH MULTICOLORED TOMATOES

Cheesecake salé aux tomates multicolores

Serves 6

Active time
1½ hours

Freezing time
5 minutes

Cooking time
20 minutes

Chilling time
1 hour

Equipment
Food processor
6 × 4-in. (10-cm) tartlet rings
Electric hand beater
Blender
Muslin cloth
3-in. (8-cm) round cookie cutter
¾-in. (2-cm) round cookie cutter

Ingredients

Cheesecake base
7 oz. (200 g) savory crackers
1 cup (3½ oz./100 g) chopped unsalted pistachios
1 stick (4 oz./120 g) butter, diced, at room temperature

Savory cheesecake filling
1 lb. (500 g) cream cheese
2 eggs
2 egg yolks
⅓ cup (80 ml) cream, minimum 35% fat
1 pinch fine salt

Glaze
2 sheets (4 g) gold bloom gelatin
1⅓ cups (320 ml) cream, minimum 35% fat
1 pinch fine salt

Clear tomato water wafers
1 lb. (500 g) beefsteak tomatoes
1 tsp (7 g) honey
2 tsp (4 g) agar agar
1 tbsp (20 g) celery salt
1 tsp (3 g) piment d'Espelette

Tomato syrup
2 oz. (50 g) fresh ginger
¾ cup (200 ml) water
¾ cup (5 oz./150 g) sugar
Scant ½ cup (100 ml) white balsamic vinegar
14 oz. (400 g) blended tomatoes
2 pinches piment d'Espelette
1 pinch fine sea salt

Topping
6 red tomatoes
6 green tomatoes
6 yellow tomatoes
3 tbsp (50 ml) best-quality olive oil
Fine salt

To serve
A few dwarf basil leaves

PREPARING THE CHEESECAKE BASE
Line a baking sheet with parchment paper. In a food processor, grind the crackers and pistachios into coarse crumbs. Add the butter and process until the crumbs have a sandy texture. Place the tartlet rings on the baking sheet and press a ¼-in. (5-mm) layer of crumbs into them. Preheat the oven to 340°F (170°C/Gas mark 3). Place in the freezer for 5 minutes, then bake for 10 minutes. Let cool to room temperature.

PREPARING THE SAVORY CHEESECAKE FILLING
Preheat the oven to 325°F (160°C/Gas just below mark 3). In a mixing bowl, whisk the cream cheese with the eggs, egg yolks, cream, and salt until smooth. Divide the filling between the tartlet rings and bake for 6–8 minutes, until just firm but not colored. Let cool to room temperature.

PREPARING THE GLAZE
Soak the gelatin in a bowl of cold water until softened. In a saucepan, bring the cream almost to a boil, squeeze the water from the gelatin, and stir into the cream until dissolved. Let cool to 95°F (35°C), then pour over the cheesecake filling. Refrigerate until set (about 15 minutes).

PREPARING THE CLEAR TOMATO WATER WAFERS
Peel the tomatoes (see technique p. 41). Blend them and strain through a muslin cloth with a weight pressed on top. You should obtain about ¾ cup (200 ml) of tomato water. In a small saucepan over medium-high heat, bring the tomato water to a boil with the honey, agar agar, celery salt, and piment d'Espelette. Pour as thin a layer as possible over a rimmed non-stick baking sheet. Chill for a few minutes, until set. Using the 3-in. (8-cm) cookie cutter, cut out 6 disks. Place them in the refrigerator until serving.

PREPARING THE TOMATO SYRUP
Peel and finely grate the ginger. In a medium saucepan over medium-high heat, bring the water to a boil with the sugar, balsamic vinegar, and ginger. Stir in the blended tomatoes and piment d'Espelette. Reduce the heat to low and let simmer until reduced by a third and syrupy. Let cool and season with salt. If the syrup is too thick, stir in a little water.

PREPARING THE TOPPING
Peel and seed the tomatoes (see technique p. 41) and cut them into disks using the ¾-in. (2-cm) cookie cutter. Season with salt and drizzle with the olive oil, then let marinate until ready to serve.

TO ASSEMBLE
Spoon a circle of tomato syrup into the center of each serving plate. Unmold the cheesecakes, arrange the tomato disks on top, and cover each one with a clear tomato water wafer. Place a few dwarf basil leaves around the edge.

TOMATO GAZPACHO

Gaspacho de tomates

Serves 6

Active time
2 hours

Chilling time
1 hour

Drying time
20 minutes

Cooking time
10 minutes

Equipment
Blender
Fine-mesh sieve
Silicone baking mat

Ingredients

Gazpacho
3 garlic cloves
2 red onions
1 yellow bell pepper
1 red bell pepper
12 Torino tomatoes, or another variety of full-flavored plum tomato
7 oz. (200 g) sandwich loaf
2 tsp (10 g) tomato paste
Scant ½ cup (100 ml) sherry vinegar
Generous ¾ cup (200 ml) fruity olive oil, divided
Fleur de sel
Freshly ground pepper

Tomato chips
3 vine tomatoes
4 tsp (20 ml) olive oil
Fleur de sel and freshly ground pepper

Melba toast
1 sandwich loaf
Piment d'Espelette
Fine sea salt
4 tsp (20 ml) olive oil

Onion chips
1 onion
Confectioners' sugar for sprinkling

To garnish and serve
1 bunch scallions
Smoked paprika

PREPARING THE GAZPACHO
Wash all the vegetables. Peel the garlic, onions, and bell peppers (see technique p. 43). Finely dice half of each pepper into brunoise (see technique p. 60) and set aside. Cut the remaining halves into large dice. Halve 1 red onion lengthwise and cut 1 half into 6 segments. Set aside. Chop the remaining onions (see technique p. 56), cut the tomatoes into large cubes, and chop the garlic. Cut the bread into large dice. Place the onions, tomatoes, garlic, and bread in a large mixing bowl and stir in the tomato paste, vinegar, and ⅔ cup (150 ml) of the olive oil. Season with salt and pepper and chill for at least 1 hour. Blend the mixture until smooth and strain through a fine-mesh sieve, pressing down to extract as much liquid as possible. Season with salt and pepper and whisk in the remaining 3 tablespoons (50 ml) olive oil.

PREPARING THE TOMATO CHIPS
Preheat the oven to 175°F (80°C/Gas at lowest possible setting). Line a baking sheet with a silicone baking mat or parchment paper. Cut the tomatoes into 12 × 1/16-in. (2-mm) slices. Season them with salt and pepper and drizzle with the olive oil. Dry out in the oven until crisp (about 10 minutes).

PREPARING THE MELBA TOAST
Increase the oven temperature to 300°F (150°C/Gas mark 2). Line two baking sheets with parchment paper. Using a serrated knife, cut 12 very thin slices of bread. Season with piment d'Espelette and salt and brush with the olive oil. Place the slices on the baking sheets, cover with another sheet of parchment paper, and bake for about 10 minutes, until golden.

PREPARING THE ONION CHIPS
Lower the oven temperature to 120°F (50°C/Gas at lowest possible setting). Peel and cut the onion into thin slices, about 1/16 in. (2 mm) thick. Spread them on a silicone baking mat or baking sheet lined with parchment paper, sprinkle them lightly with confectioners' sugar, and dry them out in the oven until a pale brown color (about 10 minutes).

PREPARING THE GARNISH
Cut the scallions into thin angled slices (see technique p. 64).

TO SERVE
Divide the bell pepper brunoise and onion segments among 6 serving glasses or bowls. Pour in the gazpacho and garnish with the sliced scallions. Sprinkle with smoked paprika and arrange the tomato chips, onion chips, and Melba toasts around.

SMOKED EGGPLANT GAZPACHO

Gaspacho d'aubergine fumée

Serves 6

Active time
45 minutes

Cooking time
30 minutes

Chilling time
1 hour

Equipment
Kitchen torch
Immersion blender
¾-in. (2-cm) round
cookie cutter

Ingredients

Gazpacho
2¼ lb. (1 kg) eggplants
7 oz. (200 g) potatoes
1 garlic clove
Scant 2½ cups (600 ml)
vegetable stock
Scant ½ cup (100 ml)
cream, minimum 35% fat
3 tbsp (50 ml) olive oil
½ tsp (1 g) ground cumin
Piment d'Espelette
Fine sea salt

Ricotta
3½ oz. (100 g) ricotta
Olive oil
Salt and freshly ground
pepper

To garnish and serve
2 yellow tomatoes
2 red tomatoes
4 red pearl onions
1 lb. 5 oz. (600 g) white
eggplants
2 slices sandwich loaf
1 garlic clove, unpeeled
2¼ tsp (10 g) clarified
butter, for frying
¾ oz. (20 g) micro basil
12 unsprayed nasturtium
leaves
12 garlic flowers
Olive oil for drizzling

PREPARING THE GAZPACHO

Wash the eggplants. Using the kitchen torch, very carefully burn the skin until charred all over (see technique p. 46). Leave until cool enough to handle before peeling off the skin and scraping the flesh into a bowl—you should have about 1 lb. 5 oz. (600 g) eggplant flesh. Wash and peel the potatoes and cut into chunks. Peel the garlic clove. In a pan over high heat, bring the vegetable stock to a boil, add the potatoes and garlic, and cook until softened. Blend with the eggplant, gradually adding the cream. Stir in the olive oil and season with cumin, piment d'Espelette, and salt. Refrigerate until well chilled.

PREPARING THE RICOTTA

Whisk the ricotta with a little olive oil until smooth. Season with salt and pepper.

PREPARING THE GARNISHES

Peel the tomatoes (see technique p. 41); if large, quarter them, otherwise you can leave them whole. Peel and halve the red onions lengthwise and cut into thick slices. Preheat the oven to 425°F (220°C/Gas mark 7), place the white eggplants on a baking sheet (cut large ones in half lengthwise), and roast for about 15 minutes. Cut into wedges. Using the cookie cutter, cut the bread into disks. Fry the bread disks with the unpeeled garlic clove in the clarified butter in a skillet over medium heat, until golden brown and crisp. Drain on paper towel.

TO SERVE

Arrange the garnishes and the ricotta in a line two-thirds of the way across each serving bowl, placing them close enough together to prevent the gazpacho running through them. Top with the micro basil, nasturtium leaves, and garlic flowers. Immediately before serving, pour the gazpacho from a jug into the larger space alongside the garnishes.

PAN-FRIED ZUCCHINI WITH WHIPPED FETA CREAM

Courgettes vertes poêlées avec chantilly de feta

Serves 6

Active time
40 minutes

Drying time
1 hour

Cooking time
1 hour

Equipment
Silicone baking mat
Pestle and mortar
or food processor
Electric hand beater
Pastry bag with a fluted
tip
Silicone baking mat
with a leaf pattern

Ingredients

Dried parsley powder
1 bunch flat-leaf parsley

Pan-fried zucchini
12 mini zucchini
12 zucchini flowers
Scant ½ cup (100 ml)
olive oil
Salt and freshly ground
pepper

Whipped feta cream
5 oz. (150 g) feta
¾ cup (200 ml) cream,
minimum 35% fat

Lacy tomato leaves
½ cup minus 1 tbsp
(1¾ oz./50 g) all-
purpose flour
Scant ¼ cup
(1¾ oz./50 g) egg white
(about 1½ whites)
3 tbsp plus 1 tsp
(1¾ oz./50 g) melted
butter
1¾ oz (50 g) tomato
paste
⅓ oz. (10 g) dried
parsley powder
(see above)
Piment d'Espelette

Mini croutons
3½ oz. (100 g) sandwich
loaf
Oil for frying

To serve
3 tbsp (50 ml) Banyuls
vinegar or sherry
vinegar
Dried parsley powder,
for dusting (see above)
A little olive oil
Lemon marigold flowers
Nasturtium leaves

PREPARING THE DRIED PARSLEY POWDER
Pick the parsley leaves from their stems, wash them, and spread them out on a silicone baking mat. Preheat the oven to 120°F (50°C/Gas at lowest possible setting) and place the parsley in the oven for 1 hour to dehydrate it. When the parsley is completely dry, reduce it to a fine powder using a pestle and mortar or food processor.

PREPARING THE PAN-FRIED ZUCCHINI
Trim the mini zucchini and boil them *à l'anglaise* until tender (see technique p. 90). Let cool, drain, and cut in 2 lengthwise. Preheat the oven to 120°F (50°C/Gas at lowest possible setting). Wash the zucchini flowers and gently pat them dry. Place on a baking sheet, brush them with oil, season with salt, and bake for 20 minutes.

PREPARING THE WHIPPED FETA CREAM
Crumble the feta and melt it with the cream over low-medium heat in a small heavy saucepan. Let cool, chill, and then whip until it holds soft peaks. Transfer to a pastry bag fitted with a fluted tip and chill in the refrigerator until ready to serve.

PREPARING THE LACY TOMATO LEAVES
Preheat the oven to 325°F (160°C/Gas mark 3). Line a baking sheet with the leaf-patterned baking mat. Combine all the ingredients and spread over the baking sheet. Bake for 6 minutes, until golden brown and crisp. Let cool on the mat until firm enough to remove, then transfer to a wire rack to cool completely.

PREPARING THE MINI CROUTONS
Cut the sandwich loaf into ⅟₁₆-in. (2-mm) dice. In a skillet over medium-high heat, fry them in a little oil until golden. Drain on paper towel and season with salt.

TO SERVE
In a small saucepan, reduce the vinegar until syrupy. Dust each serving plate with dried parsley powder and arrange the pan-fried zucchini attractively with drops of olive oil and the vinegar reduction. Pipe the feta cream onto the zucchini and garnish with the marigold flowers, nasturtium leaves, zucchini flowers, lacy tomato leaves, and mini croutons.

GOAT CHEESE AND CUCUMBER MOUSSE

Mousse de chèvre et concombre

Serves 6

Active time
1 hour

Cooling time
30 minutes

Chilling time
2½ hours

Cooking time
30 minutes

Freezing time
1½ hours

Equipment
Mandoline
6 × 2¼-in. (6-cm) round silicone molds, 1¾ in. (2 cm) deep
Juicer
Immersion blender
2-in. (5-cm) round cookie cutter

Ingredients

Pickled Persian cucumbers
2 Persian cucumbers
⅔ cup (150 ml) white wine
½ cup (125 ml) white balsamic vinegar
¼ cup (2 oz./50 g) sugar
3½ tbsp (2½ oz./75 g) honey
1 tsp coriander seeds

Cucumber tartare
½ cucumber
5 mint leaves
2 tbsp olive oil
Salt and freshly ground pepper

Goat cheese mousse
3 sheets (6 g) gold bloom gelatin
¾ cup (200 g) cream, minimum 35% fat
10 oz. (300 g) creamy full-flavored goat cheese
Salt and freshly ground pepper

Cucumber jelly
1¾ sheets (3.5 g) gelatin
2 cucumbers
10 mint leaves
¾ tsp (1.25 g) agar agar
1 tbsp plus 2 tsp (25 ml) ouzo
Scant ½ tsp (2 g) fine sea salt

Apple and cucumber dressing
9 oz. (250 g) cucumber
9 oz. (250 g) Granny Smith apples
Scant ⅓ cup (70 ml) yuzu juice
1 pinch fine sea salt
0.08 oz. (2 g) xanthan gum

To serve
Edible gold dust
12 mizuna leaves
1 green apple, peeled and cut into matchsticks
1 Persian cucumber

PREPARING THE PICKLED PERSIAN CUCUMBERS
Using a mandoline, cut the cucumbers lengthwise into 1/16-in. (1-mm) slices. In a small saucepan over medium heat, bring the wine, vinegar, sugar, and honey to a boil. Add the coriander seeds, remove from the heat, and let cool to room temperature for about 30 minutes. Pour over the cucumber slices and chill for 2 hours.

PREPARING THE CUCUMBER TARTARE
Peel the cucumber, cut it in half lengthwise, and scoop out the seeds. Cut it into brunoise (see technique p. 60). Cut the mint leaves into julienne strips (see technique p. 58), combine with the cucumber, and season with olive oil, salt, and pepper.

PREPARING THE GOAT CHEESE MOUSSE
Soak the gelatin in a bowl of cold water until softened. Bring the cream to a boil in a heavy saucepan. Roughly mash the cheese with a fork and whisk it into the cream. Squeeze the water from the gelatin and stir in until the mixture is smooth. Season with salt and pepper and pour into the silicone molds to half-fill. Spoon a little cucumber tartare on top and then pour in the remaining mousse. Freeze for 1½ hours until set. Turn the mousses out of the molds and transfer to the refrigerator to defrost.

PREPARING THE CUCUMBER JELLY
Soak the gelatin in a bowl of cold water until softened. Juice the cucumbers with the mint leaves. Weigh out about 9 oz. (250 g) of the juice and stir in the agar agar. Pour into a medium saucepan over medium-high heat and bring to a boil. Let boil for 2 minutes and remove from the heat. Squeeze the water from the gelatin and stir in until dissolved. Stir in the ouzo and salt. Pour a very thin layer of the jelly (about 1/16 in./1 mm) onto a large rimmed baking sheet and chill until set. Using the cookie cutter, cut out 6 cucumber jelly disks and place on top of the goat cheese mousses.

PREPARING THE APPLE AND CUCUMBER DRESSING
Juice the cucumber and apples, and stir in the yuzu juice and salt. Incorporate the xanthan gum using an immersion blender. Chill until ready to serve.

TO SERVE
Place a goat cheese mousse on each serving plate, or several on a plate to share, and sprinkle the gold dust over the cucumber jelly. Drain the pickled Persian cucumber slices, then roll them up and arrange them around the mousse. Add a few dots of apple and cucumber dressing and garnish with the mizuna leaves, apple matchsticks, and cucumber shaped into flowers.

MINI BELL PEPPERS WITH PIPERADE, MARBLED GLAZE, AND GAMBAS

Mini poivrons à la piperade, glacis bicolore et gambas

Serves 4

Active time
45 minutes

Cooking time
45 minutes

Equipment
Blender
Fine-mesh sieve
Wooden skewers

Ingredients

Mini bell peppers
4 yellow mini bell peppers
4 red mini bell peppers

Piperade (Basque-style stewed peppers)
7 oz. (200 g) yellow bell peppers
7 oz. (200 g) red bell peppers
2½ oz. (70 g) red onion
2 garlic cloves
3 tbsp (50 ml) olive oil
2 thyme sprigs
3 oz. (85 g) cured ham

Marbled glaze
1½ lb. (700 g) yellow bell peppers
1½ lb. (700 g) red bell peppers

Gambas
4 gambas or extra-large shrimp

PREPARING THE MINI BELL PEPPERS

Wash the bell peppers and cut off the tops with the stems attached. Scoop out the seeds, taking care not to break the pepper shells. Set the peppers and tops aside.

PREPARING THE PIPERADE

Wash, peel, seed, and chop the bell peppers. Peel the onion and cut it into ⅛-in. (3-mm) slices (see technique p. 55). Peel and chop the garlic. Heat the olive oil in a skillet over low-medium heat and sweat the onions. Add the bell peppers, garlic, and thyme. Cover with the lid and let cook gently for 30 minutes until very soft. While the peppers are cooking, dice the ham, and stir it into the pepper mixture at the last minute. Remove from the heat and let cool. Preheat the oven to 350°F (180°C/Gas mark 4). Spoon the piperade and ham into the mini bell peppers to fill them, replace the tops, place them on a baking sheet, and roast for about 10 minutes.

PREPARING THE MARBLED GLAZE

Wash the bell peppers, remove the stems and seeds, and roughly chop. Blend each color of pepper separately and strain through a fine-mesh sieve to catch all the juices. In separate saucepans over low heat, reduce the juices until syrupy. Set aside.

PREPARING THE GAMBAS

Remove the heads, and wash and reserve in the refrigerator until serving. Peel away and discard the shells, leaving the tails still attached. Make a shallow cut down the back of each gambas and pull out the dark thread (intestinal tract). Thread the gambas lengthwise onto skewers to keep their shape and ensure they remain straight. Cook in a steam oven at 195°F (90°C) or steamer for 4 minutes.

TO SERVE

Brush the gambas with the red glaze until coated. Using a small spoon, marble the red and yellow glazes on each serving plate. Place 1 red and 1 yellow stuffed mini pepper on one side of the plate with a gambas alongside. Sit a gambas head between the two peppers.

AVOCADO ON QUINOA TOAST WITH YUZU JELLY

Avocado toast

Serves 6

Active time
1 hour

Cooling time
30 minutes

Freezing time
3 hours minimum

Chilling time
15 minutes

Cooking time
40 minutes

Equipment
Ice-cream maker
Immersion blender
2 silicone baking mats
Large pipette or medium
squeeze bottle
Melon baller
Grill pan

Ingredients

Avocado sorbet
1¼ cups (300 ml) water
3½ tbsp (1½ oz./40 g)
sugar
1⁄10 oz. (2.5 g) stabilizer
(optional)
1½ oz. (40 g) glucose
powder
2 avocados
Juice of 2 limes
1 large pinch fine sea salt

Quinoa crackers
2 cups (500 ml) water
7 oz. (200 g) quinoa
Scant ½ cup
(3½ oz./100 g) egg
white (about 3 whites)
½ tsp (1.5 g) ground
cumin
1¼ cups (300 ml) olive
oil
Fine sea salt

Yuzu jelly
½ cup (125 ml) water
½ cup (125 ml) yuzu
juice
3 tbsp (1¼ oz./35 g)
sugar
2 tsp (4 g) agar agar

Crushed avocado
½ red onion
¼ fresh red chili pepper
4 avocados
Juice of ½ lime
2 tbsp (30 ml) olive oil
Fine sea salt and freshly
ground pepper

To garnish and serve
Juice of ½ lime
2 avocados
Small handful cilantro
leaves
A few slices red onion
A few slices red chili
pepper
Piment d'Espelette

PREPARING THE AVOCADO SORBET

In a small saucepan, bring the water and sugar to a boil with the stabilizer, if using, and glucose powder. Remove from the heat and let cool for 30 minutes. Halve, pit, and peel the avocados, and dice the flesh. Place in a bowl and toss with the lime juice. Pour in the syrup, stir in the salt, and transfer to an ice-cream maker. Churn according to the manufacturer's instructions and then freeze for at least 3 hours.

PREPARING THE QUINOA CRACKERS

In a saucepan, bring the water to a boil, add a little salt, and cook the quinoa according to the package instructions. Drain and, using an immersion blender, process with the egg whites and cumin to make a dough. Preheat the oven to 375°F (190°C/Gas mark 5). Roll out the dough thinly (about ⅛ in./3-4 mm thick) between two silicone baking mats, remove the top mat, and bake for 30 minutes. Let cool on a wire rack before breaking into large pieces. Heat the olive oil in a large skillet over medium-high heat and fry the pieces of cracker until crisp. Drain on paper towel and then sprinkle with salt.

PREPARING THE YUZU JELLY

In a small saucepan, bring the water and yuzu juice to a boil. Stir in the sugar and agar agar and bring to a boil again. Let boil for a minute or so, then let cool. Blend to ensure the mixture is very smooth and transfer to a pipette or squeeze bottle. Chill until serving.

PREPARING THE CRUSHED AVOCADO

Peel and finely chop the red onion (see technique p. 56). Wash the chili pepper, remove the seeds, and finely chop. Halve, pit, and peel the avocados, and crush the flesh with a fork. Stir in the lime juice, red onion, and chili pepper. Season with salt and pepper and stir in just enough olive oil to ensure the mixture is smooth but not runny. Transfer to a bowl, press plastic wrap over the surface, and chill in the refrigerator until ready to serve.

PREPARING THE GARNISH

Using the melon baller, scoop out 18 balls of crushed avocado, reserving the rest. Drizzle the balls with the lime juice to prevent them discoloring. Halve, pit, and peel the avocados. Cut the flesh lengthwise into 6 × ¾-in. (2-cm) slices. Heat a grill pan until very hot and quickly sear the avocado slices to scorch dark lines on both of their cut sides.

TO SERVE

Spread a little of the remaining crushed avocado on the quinoa crackers and arrange the avocado balls attractively on top. Add a slice of grilled avocado, a quenelle of avocado sorbet, some cilantro leaves, red onion and chili pepper slices, and a light dusting of piment d'Espelette. Finish by piping small pearls of yuzu jelly onto the toasts.

SPICY THAI RED PORK CURRY

Pâte de curry thaï pour "porc qui pique"

Serves 10

Active time
30 minutes

Cooking time
30 minutes

Equipment
Wok
Pestle and mortar
Food processor

Ingredients

Thai red curry paste
4 shallots
4 garlic cloves
3½ oz. (100 g) fresh ginger
7 oz. (200 g) lemongrass stalks
3½ oz. (100 g) cilantro roots or Thai cilantro (Chinese parsley) stems
1 tbsp coriander seeds
1 tsp cumin seeds
20 white peppercorns
7 red bird's eye chili peppers
10 red chili peppers
2 tsp finely grated kaffir lime zest

Pork and eggplant
1¾ lb. (800 g) boneless lean pork meat
4 large red chili peppers
2 eggplants
25 mini eggplants
50 Thai eggplants
8 tbsp (120 ml) sunflower oil, divided
4 tsp (20 ml) Thai red curry paste (see above)
1⅔ cups (400 ml) coconut milk
2 kaffir lime leaves (optional)
4 tsp (20 g) palm sugar
6 tbsp (90 ml) soy sauce
Fresh green peppercorns

To serve
Cilantro leaves (optional)
Thai fragrant rice (optional)

PREPARING THE THAI RED CURRY PASTE

Peel and finely chop the shallots (see technique p. 56). Peel the garlic, remove the germs, and chop the cloves. Peel and grate the ginger. Chop the lemongrass stalks and cilantro roots (see technique p. 56). Place a wok over high heat without adding any oil, add the coriander seeds, cumin seeds, and white peppercorns, and toast for about 3 minutes, until they release a fragrant, toasted aroma; shake the wok occasionally to keep the spices moving and take care not to burn them. Crush the toasted whole spices to a powder with a pestle and mortar. Using a food processor (or pestle and mortar), blend all the other ingredients together to make a paste and then add the toasted, ground spices.

PREPARING THE PORK AND EGGPLANT

Cut the pork into 2-in. (5-cm) strips. Cut the red chili peppers in half lengthwise, remove the seeds, and cut into ⅛- × 1¼-in. (3-mm × 3-cm) rings. Wash all the eggplants. Cut the ordinary eggplants into 2-in. (5-cm) strips, halve the mini eggplants, and leave the Thai eggplants whole. Place a wok over high heat, pour in half the oil, and stir-fry all the prepared eggplants. Drain, reduce the heat to low, add the remaining oil, and stir-fry the red curry paste for 30–45 seconds. Add the pork and stir-fry over high heat until the strips are browned. Add fresh green peppercorns to your taste, lower the heat to medium, and stir in the coconut milk and lime leaves, if using. Return the fried eggplants to the pan, add the chili pepper rings, and stir well. Mix in the palm sugar and soy sauce and let simmer until the sauce thickens a little. Remove from the heat.

TO SERVE

Serve sprinkled with cilantro leaves and accompany with steamed Thai fragrant rice, if wished.

LEAFY VEGETABLES AND SALAD GREENS

CHICKEN B'STILLA WITH HONEY, ALMONDS, AND SPINACH

Pastilla de volaille au miel, amandes et épinard

Serves 6

Active time
1 hour

Cooking time
45 minutes

Equipment
Food processor
8–9-in. (20–22-cm) round cake pan
Long metal skewer

Ingredients

Clarified butter
1¾ sticks (7 oz./200 g) unsalted butter

Stuffing
2 onions
4 chicken breasts
2 tbsp (2 oz./50 g) honey
½ tsp ground cinnamon
Finely grated zest of 1 orange
1 cup (3½ oz./100 g) toasted sliced almonds
Salt and freshly ground pepper

Spinach
1 garlic clove
1¼ lb. (600 g) baby spinach
Olive oil
Salt and freshly ground pepper

Sauce
1½ tbsp (1½ oz./40 g) honey
4 tsp (20 ml) sherry vinegar
Juice of 4 oranges
4 tbsp (2 oz./60 g) unsalted butter, diced and at room temperature

To assemble and serve
8 sheets brik pastry
2 hard-boiled eggs
Confectioners' sugar for dusting
4 oz. (125 g) frisée lettuce or other slightly bitter greens
4 oz. (125 g) baby spinach
12 small mint leaves
1 handful toasted whole almonds

PREPARING THE CLARIFIED BUTTER

In a heavy saucepan, melt the butter gently over low heat. Skim off the froth, then pour the clear yellow layer of clarified butter into a jug, leaving behind the milky residue.

PREPARING THE STUFFING

Peel and slice the onions (see technique p. 55). Cut the chicken breasts into thin strips. In a large saucepan over low heat, warm the honey until it foams. Add the onion and cook until the liquid from the onions has evaporated. Stir in the chicken strips and increase the heat to medium. Cook, stirring frequently, until all the liquid has evaporated. Transfer to a food processor, add the cinnamon, orange zest, and almonds, and process until smooth. Season with salt and pepper.

PREPARING THE SPINACH

Peel and crush the garlic and wash the spinach. In a large skillet over medium heat, cook the spinach with a little olive oil and the garlic until wilted. Season with salt and pepper.

ASSEMBLING THE B'STILLA

Preheat the oven to 400°F (200°C/Gas mark 6). Line the base of the cake pan with parchment paper. Brush 6 sheets of brik pastry with the clarified butter and line them one by one into the cake pan in a rosette shape, letting the sheets hang over the sides of the pan. Spoon in half the stuffing, brush another sheet of pastry with clarified butter, and lay this over the stuffing. Spread half the spinach in an even layer over the pastry. Shell and slice the eggs, arrange the slices on top, and cover with the remaining spinach. Brush the last sheet of brik pastry with the clarified butter, place it over the spinach, and spread with the remaining chicken stuffing. Fold the overhanging pastry sheets over the top to enclose the stuffing. Bake for 15 minutes or until golden brown and crisp.

PREPARING THE SAUCE

While the b'stilla is baking, warm the honey in a small saucepan over low heat until it caramelizes. Deglaze with the vinegar and let it evaporate so the sauce is slightly bitter. Stir in the orange juice, reduce until syrupy, and then whisk in the butter.

TO SERVE

Unmold the b'stilla onto a serving plate. Dust with confectioners' sugar and, protecting your hand with an oven mitt, heat a metal skewer over a flame until red hot and carefully scorch a lattice pattern on the top. Serve with a salad of frisée lettuce, baby spinach leaves, and mint leaves. Scatter with the toasted almonds and accompany with the sauce.

CHEFS' NOTES

Instead of dusting with confectioners' sugar and marking a lattice pattern, you can sprinkle over a little ground cinnamon.

BELGIAN ENDIVE AND HAM SOUFFLÉ

Soufflé aux endives et jambon

Serves 6

Active time
1 hour

Chilling time
30 minutes

Cooking time
1 hour

Equipment
7-in. (16-cm) soufflé dish,
4 in. (10 cm) deep
Hot water bath
Thermometer
Electric hand beater

Ingredients

Belgian endives
2¼ lb. (1 kg) Belgian endives
Juice of 1 lemon
Salt and freshly ground pepper

Soufflé mixture
2 tbsp (30 ml) melted butter for brushing
1 stick (4 oz./120 g) unsalted butter
1 cup (4 oz./120 g) all-purpose flour
4 cups (1 liter) whole or reduced fat milk
8 eggs
1 tbsp (15 g) fine salt
2 oz. (50 g) grated Comté cheese, or other full-flavored hard cheese
3 oz. (80 g) diced ham

To assemble
2 oz. (50 g) Comté cheese, or other full-flavored hard cheese
2 oz. (50 g) sliced ham
Kosher salt

PREPARING THE BELGIAN ENDIVES
Remove the outer leaves and any damaged ones from the endives. Trim off the base and cut the endives in half lengthwise. Remove the centers and slice finely. Place in a saucepan with the lemon juice and 2 tablespoons water, cover, and cook over low heat until tender. Season.

PREPARING THE SOUFFLÉ MIXTURE
Grease the base and sides of the soufflé dish with some of the melted butter, brushing the sides from the base to the top. Chill for 30 minutes to firm up the butter, then brush with butter again. In a medium saucepan over low heat, melt 1 stick (4 oz./120 g) butter and, using a wooden spoon, stir in the flour to make a white roux. Remove from the heat and let cool to room temperature. In a large saucepan over medium-high heat, bring the milk to a boil. Meanwhile, separate the eggs. Stir the milk gradually into the roux until smooth, add the salt, and return to medium heat. Cook for about 3 minutes, stirring constantly until you have a smooth, thickened béchamel. Remove from the heat and stir in the egg yolks one at a time. Press plastic wrap over the surface of the sauce to prevent a skin forming and set aside in a hot water bath at 145°F (63°C). Using an electric beater, whisk the egg whites until they hold soft peaks. Remove the béchamel from the water bath and stir in a little of the whisked whites to loosen it. Stir in the grated cheese, endives, and diced ham, and lightly fold in the remaining egg whites until evenly combined. Return to the heat and warm for a few minutes.

ASSEMBLING THE SOUFFLÉ
Cut both the ham and cheese into 3 diamond shapes measuring ¾ × 1 in. (1.5 × 2.5 cm). Pour the soufflé mixture into the dish to within ½ in. (1 cm) of the rim. Arrange the ham and cheese diamonds alternately in a ring on top of the soufflé. Make a bed of kosher salt in a large ovenproof saucepan and set the soufflé dish on top. Preheat the oven to 400°F (200°C/Gas mark 6). Place the saucepan over medium heat and cook for 15 minutes. Transfer the soufflé dish, still in the saucepan, to the oven and cook for about 20 minutes, until well risen and golden brown. Serve the soufflé immediately.

SALMON WITH SORREL SAUCE

Saumon à l'oseille

Serves 6

Active time
1 hour

Soaking time
10 minutes

Cooking time
10 minutes

Equipment
Fishbone tweezers

Ingredients

Salmon
2 lb. (900 g) salmon fillet
4 cups (1 liter) water
1 oz. (30 g) fine sea salt
2 tsp (10 g) sugar

Sorrel sauce
2 bunches sorrel
7 tbsp (3½ oz./100 g) unsalted butter
2 cups (500 ml) cream, minimum 35% fat
2 oz. (50 g) salmon roe
Salt and freshly ground pepper

To serve
Tiny edible flowers
Red-veined sorrel leaves

PREPARING THE SALMON

Using the tweezers, remove any tiny pin bones from the salmon, and cut the fillet into 6 × 5-oz. (150-g) portions. Place the salmon fillets in a single layer in a large dish, combine the water with the salt and sugar to make a brining liquid, and pour it over the salmon. Let the salmon marinate for 10 minutes and then drain. In a non-stick skillet, cook the salmon fillets over medium heat for 4–5 minutes, turning the fillets once. The flesh should flake easily but still be translucent in the center.

PREPARING THE SORREL SAUCE

Wash and dry the sorrel leaves. In a sauté pan over medium heat, melt the butter and cook the sorrel leaves until wilted. Stir in the cream and salmon roe, and season with salt and pepper.

TO SERVE

Spoon the sorrel sauce into 6 deep serving plates and place a salmon fillet in the center of each one. Garnish with tiny edible flowers and red-veined sorrel leaves.

SWISS CHARD AND SCALLOP GREEN CURRY

Curry vert de blettes et noix de Saint-Jacques

Serves 6

Active time
1½ hours

Infusing time
20 minutes

Cooking time
30 minutes

Equipment
Pestle and mortar
Food-safe disposable gloves
Fine-mesh sieve
Immersion blender

Ingredients

Green curry paste
1 tbsp coriander seeds, toasted
10 white peppercorns
1 tbsp cumin seeds
1 tsp ground turmeric
10 fresh green bird's eye chili peppers
7 large fresh green chili peppers
¼ oz. (6 g) galangal root
½ oz. (15 g) Thai shallot
¾ oz. (20 g) garlic cloves
¼ oz. (6 g) lemongrass
Stalks of 1 bunch cilantro
1 tbsp (15 g) salt
Finely grated zest of 1 kaffir lime
1 tbsp shrimp paste (prawn sauce)

Green curry sauce
2 cups (500 ml) coconut cream, divided
1½ oz. (40 g) green curry paste (see above)
1–2 tbsp (15–30 ml) fish sauce
1 tbsp (15 g) palm sugar
¼ oz. (6 g) Thai basil leaves
1 kaffir lime leaf
5 Swiss chard leaves

Swiss chard
1 bunch Swiss chard
1 garlic clove
3 tbsp (50 ml) olive oil
2 cups (500 ml) white chicken stock
1 thyme sprig
2 tbsp (1 oz./30 g) butter

To serve
2 tbsp (30 ml) olive oil
18 scallops with their coral
1 red bird's eye chili pepper, finely sliced
Leaves from ¼ bunch Thai basil
18 shavings fresh coconut

PREPARING THE GREEN CURRY PASTE

Using a pestle and mortar, crush the coriander seeds, peppercorns, and cumin seeds with the turmeric. Wearing disposable gloves to protect your hands, wash both types of chili peppers, halve them, and scrape out the seeds. Finely dice the chilis and reduce them to a paste by crushing in the pestle and mortar. Peel the galangal, Thai shallot, and garlic and finely chop them with the lemongrass and cilantro stalks. Gradually add them to the mortar with the salt and crush. Finally, add the kaffir lime zest and shrimp paste and crush everything together to make a smooth paste.

PREPARING THE GREEN CURRY SAUCE

In a saucepan over medium-high heat, bring half the coconut cream to a boil. Reduce the heat to low and stir in the green curry paste. Simmer for 5 minutes, drizzle in the remaining coconut cream, and simmer for an additional 15 minutes. Stir in the fish sauce and palm sugar and bring to a boil again. Remove from the heat, add the basil and kaffir lime leaf, and let infuse for 20 minutes. Strain the sauce through a fine-mesh sieve into a bowl. Wash and add the chard leaves and, using an immersion blender, blend until smooth and a vivid green color. Strain again and reserve at room temperature.

PREPARING THE SWISS CHARD

Cut off the white stalks from the leaves. Using a vegetable peeler, peel the stalks to remove the tough fibers at the base, and cut them into roughly 6-in. (15-cm) lengths. Wash the leaves and dry them in a salad spinner. Peel the garlic clove but leave it whole. In a skillet over medium heat, sweat the stalks in the olive oil without letting them color. Pour in the chicken stock and add the garlic clove and thyme sprig. At the last minute, melt the butter in another skillet and briefly cook the leaves until wilted.

TO SERVE

Heat the olive oil in a skillet over high heat. Separate the scallops and corals and sauté both until the scallops are golden on both sides and the corals lightly cooked. Pour the green curry sauce into serving bowls and arrange the scallops, corals, chard stalks, and leaves attractively on top. Garnish with the red bird's eye chili pepper slices, Thai basil leaves, and the coconut shavings.

CARDOON QUICHE WITH WALNUTS AND CONFIT GIBLETS

Quiche de cardons, noix et gésiers confits

Serves 6

Active time
1 hour

Chilling time
50 minutes

Cooking time
50 minutes

Equipment
Food-safe
disposable gloves

6 oblong tart frames,
6 in. (15 cm) long
and 1½ in. (4 cm) wide

Ingredients

Pastry

1 cup plus 2 tbsp
(5 oz./150 g) all-purpose
flour

1 cup (3½ oz./100 g)
ground walnuts

1 stick plus 2 tsp
(4½ oz./125 g) butter,
chilled and diced

1 egg beaten with 4 tsp
(20 ml) water

Fine sea salt

Cardoon ragout

2 bunches cardoons

Juice of 1 lemon

Scant ½ cup
(1¾ oz./50 g) all-
purpose flour

4 cups (1 liter) water

Coarse sea salt

7 oz. (200 g)
confit giblets

Scant 1 cup
(3½ oz./100 g) fresh
walnuts

½ bunch flat-leaf
parsley

3 tbsp (2 oz./50 g)
butter

Scant ½ cup (100 ml)
Jura vin jaune

Salt and freshly ground
pepper

Cream filling

1 cup (250 ml) cream,
minimum 35% fat

2 eggs

2 egg yolks

Freshly grated nutmeg

Salt and freshly ground
pepper

To serve

10 oz. (300 g)
watercress

3 tbsp (50 ml) walnut oil,
divided

3 tbsp (50 ml) brown
chicken *jus*

1¼ cups (300 ml)
watercress coulis
(optional)

PREPARING THE PASTRY

On a clean work surface, mix the all-purpose flour with the ground walnuts. Rub the butter into the flour and add salt. Make a well in the center, pour in the beaten egg and water, and work into the flour mixture. Push down the dough with the palm of your hand, pushing it away from you over the work surface. Do this twice, and then shape the dough into a ball, cover in plastic wrap, and chill for 30 minutes.

PREPARING THE CARDOON RAGOUT

Protecting your hands with disposable gloves, peel the cardoons, and cut 1 bunch into small sticks and the other into thinly sliced disks. Place in a bowl of cold water and add the lemon juice to prevent them discoloring. In a large saucepot, whisk the flour into the water. Bring to a boil, stirring constantly to make a white bouillon, and add the salt and cardoons. Cut a disk of parchment paper the same diameter as the saucepan, place on top, and cook for about 20 minutes, until the cardoon sticks and disks are tender. Drain, rinse under cold water, and set aside. Cut the giblets into 1/16-in. (2-mm) slices and chop the walnuts. Wash the parsley, set aside a few leaves for garnish, and chop the rest (see technique p. 54). In a sauté pan or skillet over medium-high heat, melt the butter and sauté the giblets. Add the cardoon sticks and walnuts and deglaze with the Jura wine. When the wine has reduced, stir in the chopped parsley and season with salt and pepper.

PREPARING THE CREAM FILLING

In a mixing bowl, beat all the ingredients together.

TO ASSEMBLE AND SERVE

Set the oblong tart frames on a baking sheet lined with parchment paper. Roll the dough out, line into the frames, and chill for 20 minutes. Preheat the oven to 325°F (160°C/Gas mark 3) and blind-bake the pastry cases for 10 minutes. Let cool. Divide the cardoon ragout between the pastry cases and pour in the cream filling until they are half-full. Bake for 20 minutes until the filling has set (check with the tip of a knife). Sort through the watercress, discarding any tough stalks and reserving only the greenest leaves. Rinse thoroughly and dry on paper towel. Transfer the quiches to serving plates and carefully lift off the frames. Arrange the watercress and cardoon disks on top, season with salt and pepper, and drizzle with a few drops of walnut oil and a little chicken *jus*. Brush the reserved parsley leaves with walnut oil and add to each plate, together with a few drops of watercress coulis, if using.

LAYERED ARUGULA PISTOU, POINTED CABBAGE, AND GRILLED AVOCADO

Feuille à feuille de pistou de roquette, chou pointu et avocat grillé

Serves 6

Active time
1 hour

Cooking time
25 minutes + 1 hour–
overnight for the garlic
(see Chefs' Notes)

Equipment
Fine-mesh sieve
Blender
Grill pan
3- × 7-in. (8- × 18-cm) cake
frame
Pastry bag
Pipette

Ingredients

Garlic oil
1 head garlic
1¼ cups
(300 ml) grapeseed oil

Arugula pistou
7 oz. (200 g) arugula
2 tbsp (30 ml) garlic oil
(see above)
2 tbsp (30 ml) grapeseed
oil
2 tbsp (30 ml) extra
virgin olive oil
Salt and pepper

**Pointed cabbage
and avocado terrine**
1 large pointed cabbage
2 Hass avocados

**Honey-mustard
condiment**
2 oz. (50 g) whole-
grained Meaux mustard
1 oz. (25 g) acacia
or multi-floral honey

Buttermilk curds
1¼ cups (300 ml)
buttermilk
2 tbsp (30 ml) lemon
juice
1 pinch salt

Buttermilk coulis
1½ tbsp (½ oz. /15 g)
cornstarch
¾ cup (200 ml)
buttermilk

To serve
Arugula leaves
Gray fleur de sel,
or other gray sea salt
flakes

CHEFS' NOTES

To make the garlic oil on the stovetop,
wrap the garlic and oil in a tightly sealed
foil package and place in a saucepan
of barely simmering water for 1 hour,
letting it float on top of the water.

PREPARING THE GARLIC OIL
Preheat the oven to 140°F (60°C/Gas at lowest possible setting). Separate the cloves of garlic and crush them with their skins left on. Place the garlic in a small ovenproof dish, spoon over the grapeseed oil, and place in the oven for 12 hours or overnight. Strain the oil through a fine-mesh sieve and set aside.

PREPARING THE ARUGULA PISTOU
Blend the arugula with the three oils until smooth. Season with salt and pepper.

PREPARING THE POINTED CABBAGE AND AVOCADO TERRINE
Remove the leaves from the cabbage carefully, so each one stays whole. Roast them one at a time on a grill pan, pressing them down with a metal roasting pan. Halve the unpeeled avocados and remove the pits. Cut into thick slices and roast them on a grill pan before removing the skin. Cut the roasted cabbage leaves into half lengthwise, removing the ribs. Set the cake frame on a baking sheet lined with parchment paper. Brush the frame with a little of the garlic oil and layer 3 cabbage leaves at the bottom, seasoning each one with salt and pepper. Place another on top and spread with a layer of arugula pistou. Top with avocado slices, ensuring there are no gaps between them, and then another layer of pistou, reserving a little for the honey-mustard condiment. Add 4 more layers of cabbage leaves, pressing down on the final layer to flatten the surface.

PREPARING THE HONEY-MUSTARD CONDIMENT
In a mixing bowl, whisk the remaining pistou with the mustard and honey. Transfer to a pastry bag.

PREPARING THE BUTTERMILK CURDS
In a saucepan over low heat, bring the buttermilk and lemon juice to a boil with the salt. Drain through a fine-mesh sieve and collect the curds, which have a similar texture to ricotta cheese.

PREPARING THE BUTTERMILK COULIS
In a saucepan, whisk the cornstarch into the buttermilk until smooth. Whisking constantly over medium heat, bring to a boil until thickened. Transfer to a pipette.

TO SERVE
Cut the terrine into ¾-in. (1.5-cm) slices and brown them on a grill pan. Arrange the slices on serving plates and top with the buttermilk curds and arugula leaves seasoned with garlic oil and fleur de sel. Pipe dots of the honey-mustard condiment and buttermilk coulis around the slices.

TROPICAL ROMAINE SALAD

Salade romaine exotique

Serves 6

Active time
30 minutes

Freezing time
5 minutes

Cooking time
15 minutes

Equipment
2-in. (5-cm) round cookie cutter

Ingredients
3 hearts romaine lettuce
3 chicken breasts

Coating
2/3 cup (3½ oz./100 g) cornstarch
3 tbsp (50 ml) soy sauce
4 tsp (20 ml) roasted sesame seed oil
2 beaten eggs
3½ oz. (100 g) satay sauce
10 oz. (300 g) panko bread crumbs

Tropical vinaigrette
1 red bell pepper
4 passion fruit
3 limes
1 bunch Chinese scallions
1 bunch cilantro
1 green mango
1 yellow-skinned mango
1/3 oz. (10 g) fresh ginger
1/3 cup (2 oz./50 g) unsalted peanuts
3/4 cup (200 ml) unroasted sesame oil

Cheddar lace
7 oz. (200 g) Cheddar cheese

To serve
2/3 cup (150 ml) peanut oil
Juice of 1 lime
A few cilantro leaves

Wash the romaine hearts (see technique p. 28), separate the leaves, and dry on sheets of paper towel. Refrigerate until needed. Butterfly the chicken breasts, rinse under cold water, and place between two sheets of parchment paper. Using a rolling pin, beat lightly to flatten, then place in the freezer for 5 minutes. Using the cookie cutter, cut them into disks.

PREPARING THE COATING
Spread the cornstarch on a plate. In a shallow bowl, whisk together the soy sauce, sesame oil, and eggs. In another bowl, stir the satay sauce into the panko. Coat the chicken disks with the cornstarch, shaking off any excess, dip them in the soy sauce mixture, and then in the satay-panko mixture, pressing it on so that it sticks well. Refrigerate until needed.

PREPARING THE TROPICAL DRESSING
Peel the bell pepper (see technique p. 43), seed, and finely dice. Cut the passion fruit in half and scoop out the seeds and juice into a bowl. Wash and finely grate the zest and juice the limes. Wash the scallions and cut into angled slices (see technique p. 64) and chop the cilantro (see technique p. 54). Peel the mangos, cut the flesh away from the stone, and dice into brunoise (see technique p. 60). Peel and grate the ginger and chop the peanuts. Combine all the ingredients in a bowl and stir in the sesame oil.

PREPARING THE CHEDDAR LACE
Grate the Cheddar and, working in batches, melt the cheese in a large non-stick skillet over medium-high heat until it turns crisp with a lace-like appearance. Remove from the skillet, cool, and break into pieces.

TO SERVE
Heat the oil in a large skillet over medium-high heat and fry the chicken disks until golden, turning them occasionally so they color evenly. Remove from the heat and season with the lime juice. Arrange the lettuce leaves on serving plates, top with a fried chicken disk, and tuck a piece of Cheddar lace in between. Drizzle with the tropical vinaigrette and garnish with a few cilantro leaves.

BRAISED LETTUCE WITH SMOKED BUTTER SABAYON

Sucrine braisée, sabayon au beurre fumé

Serves 6

Active time
20 minutes

Smoking time
2 hours

Cooking time
1 hour

Equipment
Smoker or food-grade hay
Hot water bath
Thermometer
Siphon + 1 cartridge

Ingredients

Smoked butter
2⅔ sticks (10½ oz./300 g) unsalted butter

Braised lettuce
1 butter lettuce
Distilled white vinegar
6 little gem lettuces
½ carrot
½ onion
1 bouquet garni, including leek greens, thyme, bay leaf, and celery leaves, tied together with kitchen twine
3 tbsp (2 oz./50 g) butter
1⅔ cups (400 ml) white veal stock

Smoked butter sabayon
5 eggs
2 egg yolks
3 tbsp (50 ml) water
Prepared smoked butter (see above)
½ cup (4 oz./120 g) Greek yogurt
Salt and freshly ground pepper

To serve
1 tbsp puffed buckwheat
Purple garlic flower petals
Tiny chervil leaves

PREPARING THE SMOKED BUTTER

Place the butter in a smoker for 2 hours. Alternatively, put it in a pot with two large handfuls of hay and carefully set the hay alight; cover with the lid immediately to extinguish the flames and trap the smoke. Place the pot in the oven, which should be switched off with the door closed, for 2 hours.

PREPARING THE BRAISED LETTUCE

Remove the outer leaves and any damaged ones from the butter lettuce, leaving the rest whole. Wash several times in water with vinegar added (see technique p. 28). In a saucepan of boiling salted water, blanch the whole lettuce for 2–3 minutes (see technique p. 88). Drain, refresh briefly under cold water, drain again, and squeeze well with your hands to remove excess water. Remove the 6 largest leaves to wrap the little gem lettuces and set aside. In a pot of boiling salted water, blanch the little gem lettuces. Drain, refresh under cold water, drain again, and squeeze to remove the excess water. Preheat the oven to 350°F (180°C/Gas mark 4). Wash and peel the carrot and onion halves. Cut into paysanne (see technique p. 61) and tie the ingredients for the bouquet garni together. In a large ovenproof sauté pan over medium heat, melt the butter and sweat the carrot and onion. Arrange the little gem lettuces in a single layer on top, pour in the veal stock, and add the bouquet garni. Place a disk of parchment paper the same size as the diameter of the pan over the vegetables and cover with a lid. Bake in the oven for 45 minutes, until tender when pierced with the tip of a knife. Drain the lettuces over a bowl, pressing on them to remove excess liquid, and reserve the cooking juices. Neatly roll each little gem lettuce in a butter lettuce leaf, return to the sauté pan, and cook with about ⅔ cup (150 ml) of the cooking juices until glossy.

PREPARING THE SMOKED BUTTER SABAYON

In a heatproof mixing bowl, beat together the eggs, egg yolks, and water. Sit over a hot water bath and whisk until the mixture thickens and reaches 180°F (82°C). Melt the smoked butter and gradually whisk it into the egg mixture. Stir in the yogurt and season with salt and pepper. Transfer to a siphon and fit with a gas cartridge.

TO SERVE

Dispense a generous amount of smoked butter sabayon from the siphon into each deep serving plate. Place a little gem lettuce parcel on top and garnish attractively with the puffed buckwheat, purple garlic flower petals, and tiny chervil leaves.

WATERCRESS COULIS WITH CREAMED ONIONS

Coulis de cresson

Serves 6

Preparation time
1 hour

Cooking time
45 minutes

Equipment
Immersion blender

Teardrop cookie cutter (or other elongated shape)

Ingredients

Watercress coulis
1 bunch watercress
4 cups (1 liter) cold water with a dash of vinegar added
Salt

Creamed onions
3 sweet onions, such as Vidalia or Walla Walla
4 tsp (20 g) butter
2 cups (500 ml) white chicken stock
3 egg yolks
1 egg
2 cups (500 ml) cream, minimum 35% fat
Salt and freshly ground pepper

Toast
6 wafer-thin slices from a sandwich loaf
Scant ½ cup (100 ml) melted clarified butter
Fine salt

To serve
2 tsp (10 g) caviar
A few watercress sprigs

PREPARING THE WATERCRESS COULIS

Wash the watercress in the cold water with vinegar added (see technique p. 30). Remove the stalks and blanch the leaves in a saucepan of boiling salted water until wilted (see technique p. 88). Drain and immediately immerse in a bowl of ice water so the leaves remain bright green. Using an immersion blender, process the leaves until smooth. The coulis can be served hot or cold.

PREPARING THE CREAMED ONIONS

Peel the onions and finely chop them. Melt the butter in a Dutch oven over medium heat, add the onions, and sweat them until they are translucent. Season with salt and pepper, pour in the stock, and cook until the onions are very soft. Preheat the oven to 175°F (80°C/Gas mark ¼). Beat the egg yolks, egg, and cream together, add to the onion mixture, and process until smooth using an immersion blender. Transfer to the oven, cover, and bake for about 30 minutes.

PREPARING THE TOAST

Increase the oven temperature to 325°F (160°C/Gas mark 3). Season the bread slices with salt and brush with the clarified butter. Place on a baking sheet and toast in the oven until crisp. Cut into teardrop (or other elongated) shapes using the cookie cutter.

TO SERVE

Spoon a little of the creamed onions into the center of each soup plate and pour the hot or cold watercress coulis around it. Place a teardrop-shaped toast in each bowl, on top of the creamed onions. Add a little caviar and garnish with watercress sprigs.

GRILLED TREVISO, GORGONZOLA RAVIOLI, AND PANCETTA

Trévise grillée, raviole de gorgonzola et pancetta

Serves 6

Active time
1 hour

Chilling time
1 hour

Cooking time
20 minutes

Equipment
Stand mixer
Pasta machine
3-in. (8-cm) round cookie cutter
Grill pan

Ingredients

Turmeric-flavored ravioli dough
1²/₃ cups (7 oz./200 g) all-purpose flour
2 eggs
2 pinches fine sea salt
2 tsp (10 ml) olive oil
1 tsp ground turmeric

Squid ink ravioli dough
1²/₃ cups (7 oz./200 g) all-purpose flour
2 eggs
2 pinches fine sea salt
2 tsp (10 ml) olive oil
½ tsp (2 g) squid ink

Ravioli stuffing
14 oz. (400 g) gorgonzola

Grilled Treviso
2 heads Treviso (or red endives, or radicchio)
4 tbsp (60 ml) olive oil
Scant ½ cup (100 ml) ratafia
Salt and freshly ground pepper

To garnish and serve
2 tbsp (20 g) Zante currants
2 tbsp (10 g) pine nuts
12 slices pancetta
12 pearl onions
Olive oil
2 oz. (50 g) wild arugula
1¼ cups (300 ml) watercress coulis
Piment d'Espelette

PREPARING THE TURMERIC-FLAVORED RAVIOLI DOUGH

In the bowl of a stand mixer fitted with the dough hook, knead all the ingredients together until you obtain a smooth dough. Shape into a ball, cover in plastic wrap, and chill for 1 hour.

PREPARING THE SQUID INK RAVIOLI DOUGH

Follow the instructions for the turmeric-flavored dough, substituting the squid ink for the turmeric, and chill for 1 hour.

PREPARING THE RAVIOLI

Using a fork, roughly mash the gorgonzola. Using a pasta machine, roll each dough separately into sheets 4–4¾ in. (10–12 cm) wide. Cut the squid ink dough into tagliatelle strips, brush lightly with water, and stick them at regular intervals to the turmeric dough sheets. Pass through the pasta machine and cut into 3-in. (8-cm) rounds using the cookie cutter. Spoon a little gorgonzola into the center of half of the rounds, dampen the dough edges, and place another round on top, pressing the edges together to seal. Reserve in the refrigerator.

PREPARING THE GRILLED TREVISO

Wash and quarter the Treviso lengthwise, coat in olive oil, and season with salt and pepper. Heat a grill pan over high heat and grill the Treviso on all sides until cooked but still crisp. Deglaze the pan with the ratafia, transfer the Treviso to a dish, and pour over the pan juices.

PREPARING THE GARNISH

Soak the currants in warm water until plump, then drain. Preheat the oven to 300°F (150°C/Gas mark 2). Line a baking sheet with parchment paper, spread the pine nuts on it, and toast for 5 minutes. Set the oven to broil and broil the pancetta slices (or do this in a skillet). Peel and halve the pearl onions lengthwise, sauté them in a little olive oil, and mix with the currants.

TO SERVE

In a large saucepan of salted boiling water, cook the ravioli for 3 minutes. Drain and drizzle with a little olive oil. Arrange them attractively on serving plates with the Treviso, pancetta, pine nuts, pearl onion halves and currants, and arugula. Add a few drops of watercress coulis to each plate and sprinkle over a little piment d'Espelette.

LAMB AND LEMON STUFFED VINE LEAVES

Feuilles de vigne à l'agneau et zeste de citron

Serves 10

Active time
1 hour

Cooking time
30 minutes

Ingredients

Stuffing
1 onion
7 oz. (200 g) lean lamb (from the leg), or ground lamb
¼ bunch flat-leaf parsley
Sunflower oil
2 lemons
1 cup (7 oz./200 g) long-grain rice
Salt and freshly ground pepper

Vine leaves
40–50 vine leaves
Sunflower oil
2 cups (500 ml) water, vegetable stock, or light brown lamb stock
Fine sea salt

Yogurt sauce
1 garlic clove
1 cup (9 oz./250 g) plain yogurt
3 tbsp (40 ml) extra virgin olive oil
¼ bunch micro cilantro cress (optional)
Salt and freshly ground pepper

PREPARING THE STUFFING

Peel and finely chop the onion (see technique p. 56). If using unground lamb, cut it into fine dice using a sharp knife. Wash and chop the parsley (see technique p. 54). In a sauté pan over medium heat, sweat the onion in a little sunflower oil. Finely grate the zest and cut the lemons into slices. Reserve the slices for cooking the vine leaves. In a mixing bowl, combine the lamb, rice, a little sunflower oil, the sweated onion, parsley, and lemon zest. Season with salt and pepper.

PREPARING THE VINE LEAVES

Prepare a bowl of water with ice cubes added. Bring a saucepan of salted water to a boil, add the vine leaves, and blanch for 3 seconds (see technique p. 88). Drain and refresh in the ice water to prevent the leaves cooking further. Line the base of a large pot with the reserved lemon slices and cover with a layer of vine leaves to prevent the stuffed vine leaves burning. Place a vine leaf on the worktop and spoon a little stuffing into the center. Fold the sides of the leaf over the stuffing and roll up, taking care not to roll too tightly; otherwise, the stuffed leaf may burst when the rice swells as it cooks. Repeat with the remaining vine leaves until all the stuffing has been used. Place the stuffed leaves side by side in the pot, without packing them together too tightly, arranging them in layers, if necessary. Pour in the water, vegetable stock, or lamb stock, set a plate a little smaller than the diameter of the pot on top of the leaves, with a weight on the plate. Cook over low heat for about 20 minutes or until all the water has been absorbed.

PREPARING THE YOGURT SAUCE

Peel and crush the garlic and combine in a bowl with the yogurt. Season with salt and pepper, and then whisk in most of the oil. Spoon into a serving bowl and drizzle with the remaining oil. Sprinkle over the micro cilantro cress, if using.

TO SERVE

Arrange the stuffed vine leaves in a serving dish and garnish with the cooked lemon slices. Accompany with the yogurt sauce for dipping.

CHEFS' NOTES

If you wish, you can cook the stuffed vine leaves in exactly the same way in a rice cooker.

BÒ BÚN WITH BEEF AND SHRIMP

Bò bún au bœuf et aux crevettes

Serves 10

Active time
2 hours

Cooking time
30 minutes

Equipment
Pot with deep-frying basket or fryer
Wok
Skimmer

Ingredients

Bò bún
9 oz. (250 g) rice noodles
Olive oil
1 lb. (500 g) sirloin (rump) steak
Oyster sauce
1 onion
Salt

Coconut sauce
14 fl. oz. (400 ml) coconut milk
1 bunch Chinese garlic chives with flowers
Salt

Spring rolls
10 oz. (300 g) lean pork shoulder
1 carrot
1 zucchini
1 shallot
20 raw shrimp
1 egg, separated
20 square spring roll wrappers
Oil for frying
Salt and freshly ground pepper

To serve
Lettuce
Mint leaves
3½ oz. (100 g) soybean sprouts
Chopped peanuts for sprinkling
Scant ½ cup (100 ml) nuoc cham (Vietnamese dipping sauce)

PREPARING THE BÒ BÚN

In a saucepan of boiling salted water, blanch the noodles. Drain, refresh briefly under cold water, and toss them in a little olive oil. Cut the steak into thin strips, toss them in oyster sauce so they are well coated, and drizzle with a little olive oil. Peel and chop the onion (see technique p. 56). Heat a little olive oil in a wok and stir-fry the onion over high heat. Add the sliced steak and stir-fry until browned.

PREPARING THE COCONUT SAUCE

In a small saucepan over low heat, warm the coconut milk. Wash and chop or snip the chives (see Chefs' Notes p. 54) and stir into the saucepan with a little salt to season.

PREPARING THE SPRING ROLLS

Chop the pork into small dice. Cut the carrot and zucchini into julienne strips (see technique p. 58) and peel and finely chop the shallot (see technique p. 56). Peel the shrimp, remove the heads and tails, and cut into ¼-in. (5-mm) dice. Combine the pork, carrot, zucchini, and shallot in a mixing bowl, lightly break up the egg white with a fork, and stir in with the shrimp. Season the stuffing generously with salt and pepper. Place a spring roll wrapper on the worktop with one corner facing you. Spoon a little of the stuffing about 2 in. (5 cm) from the corner, roll up the wrapper tightly around the filling to half-way, and fold the sides inward. Roll to the end, brushing the tip of the wrapper with a little egg yolk to stick it in place. Heat the oil in a fryer to 350°F (180°C) and deep-fry the spring rolls for 6–7 minutes, until crisp and golden brown; do this in two batches to avoid lowering the temperature of the oil. Drain with a skimmer onto a plate lined with paper towel.

TO SERVE

Arrange the lettuce, mint leaves, and soybean sprouts in one or more serving bowls. Top with the chopped peanuts and then add the rice noodles, stir-fried beef, and spring rolls cut into pieces. Serve with the coconut sauce to drizzle over and the nuoc cham for dipping.

CHEFS' NOTES

If you make the spring rolls about 1½ hours before frying,
the egg yolk will have time to dry,
which will prevent them opening as they cook.

STEM AND BULB VEGETABLES

GREEN ASPARAGUS WITH PARSLEY AND POMELO

Asperges vertes, persil et pomelos

Serves 6

Preparation
1 hour

Drying time
12 hours

Cooking time
10 minutes

Equipment
Food processor
Blender
Hot water bath
Skimmer
Electric hand beater
2 parchment paper
cones or pipettes

Ingredients

Black olive powder
9 oz. (250 g) pitted
black olives

Green asparagus
18 green asparagus
spears
2½ tsp (10 g) coarse
sea salt for every 4 cups
(1 liter) boiling water
Scant ½ cup (100 ml)
olive oil

Chlorophyll reduction
2 bunches flat-leaf
parsley
Ice cubes

Pomelo reduction
1 pomelo

Mayonnaise
2 tsp (10 g) Dijon
mustard
3 egg yolks
¾ cup (200 ml)
grapeseed oil
Fleur de sel
Freshly ground pepper

Dried parsley
Oil for coating the leaves
Fine sea salt

To serve
1 oz. (30 g) marigold
leaves
1 oz. (30 g) purple garlic
flowers
Diced flesh of 1 pomelo
Melba toast (see recipe
p. 116)

PREPARING THE BLACK OLIVE POWDER
Preheat the oven to 140°F (60°C/Gas at lowest possible setting). Line a baking sheet with parchment paper, spread the olives on it, and dry out in the oven for 12 hours. Grind to a powder in a food processer and then sift.

PREPARING THE ASPARAGUS
Prepare the asparagus and tie in bundles with kitchen twine (see technique p. 38). Bring a saucepan of water, with salt added according to the volume of water, to a boil and cook the bundles for about 3–5 minutes (see technique p. 90), depending on the thickness of the asparagus: to test for doneness, carefully squeeze the tip of a spear with your fingers to check if it gives. Refresh in a bowl of ice water, drain, and drizzle with the olive oil.

PREPARING THE CHLOROPHYLL REDUCTION
Wash the parsley, pick off 18 leaves (reserving the remaining leaves for the dried parsley), and blend these with a few ice cubes and 2 cups (500 ml) water. Set a dish towel securely over a bowl, pour the liquid into it, and twist and squeeze the cloth to extract the juice. Pour the juice into a hot water bath over medium heat and cook until a green mousse-like foam (the chlorophyll) rises to the surface. Lift this off using a skimmer and set aside.

PREPARING THE POMELO REDUCTION
Squeeze the pomelo juice into a small saucepan and simmer until it is reduced to a syrup.

PREPARING THE MAYONNAISE
Whisk the mustard and egg yolks together, season with salt and pepper, and then slowly whisk in the oil in a thin drizzle until emulsified and thickened. Divide the mayonnaise between two small bowls. Stir the chlorophyll reduction into one and the pomelo reduction into the other. Transfer to parchment paper piping cones or pipettes.

PREPARING THE DRIED PARSLEY
Coat the reserved parsley leaves with oil. Line a plate with microwave safe plastic wrap and place the leaves on it. Season with salt and cover with another plate. Microwave at 900 W for 30 seconds or until the leaves have dried. Remove the top plate and let them dry completely.

TO SERVE
Place the asparagus on a rack set over a baking sheet or board and, using the parchment paper cones or pipettes, pipe stripes of each mayonnaise over them. Dust the plates with the olive powder and arrange the asparagus spears side by side on top. Decorate with the marigold leaves, dried parsley, and purple garlic flowers. Scatter over small pieces of diced pomelo flesh and add Melba toast cut into disks.

GRILLED LEEKS AND CLAM SALPICON IN MARINIERE SAUCE

Poireau grillé en marinière de coquillages, salmigondis de couteaux et vernis

Serves 6

Active time
1 hour

Cooking time
45 minutes

Equipment
Fine-mesh sieve

Ingredients

Clams
6 Venus clams
12 razor clams

Mariniere sauce
1 shallot
¼ bunch thyme
¾ cup (200 ml) white wine
2 cups (500 ml) apple juice

Browned butter sauce
2 shallots
¾ cup (200 ml) cider vinegar
7 tbsp (3½ oz./100 g) lightly salted butter

Leeks
7 tbsp (3½ oz./100 g) lightly salted butter
3 leeks

To serve
1 Royal Gala apple or other crisp tart apple
½ bunch chives
¾ oz. (20 g) chickweed
¾ oz. (20 g) apple blossom cress

PREPARING THE CLAMS
Open the Venus clams and remove the coral. Open the razor clams and extract the flesh. Cut both into very fine dice, keeping them separate. Reserve in the refrigerator.

PREPARING THE MARINIERE SAUCE
Place 6 razor clam shells in a saucepan of water and bring to a boil to clean them. They will be used when the dish is assembled for serving. Peel and chop the shallot (see technique p. 56). Place all the remaining shells in a large saucepan. Wash the thyme sprigs and add to the pan with the chopped shallot and white wine. Cover with the lid, bring to a boil, and simmer for 5–10 minutes. Strain the cooking liquid through a fine-mesh sieve, pour into a saucepan, and boil to reduce slightly. In another saucepan, bring the apple juice to a boil, and simmer until syrupy. Stir the mariniere sauce into the apple syrup.

PREPARING THE BROWNED BUTTER SAUCE
Peel and finely chop the shallots (see technique p. 56). Simmer them in a skillet with the vinegar until the vinegar has evaporated completely. Meanwhile, melt the butter in a saucepan over medium-low heat until it browns but do not let it darken too much. Once the vinegar has evaporated, stir the browned butter into the shallots.

PREPARING THE LEEKS
Clarify the butter by melting it gently in a heavy saucepan over low heat. Skim off the froth, then pour the clear yellow layer of clarified butter into a jug, leaving behind the milky residue. Wash the leeks, cut off the white parts, and cut in half lengthwise, keeping the small roots at the base. The green parts can be used for another recipe. In a saucepan of boiling water, blanch the white parts (see technique p. 88). Heat the clarified butter in a large skillet and, when sizzling, add the leek halves, cut sides down, and fry until browned.

TO SERVE
Peel and core the apple and cut the flesh into brunoise (see technique p. 60). Wash and chop or snip the chives (see Chefs' Notes p. 54). Just before serving, gently warm the diced razor clams to enhance their whiteness and combine with the diced Venus clams, apple, and chives to make the clam salpicon. Spoon the salpicon into the cleaned razor clam shells. Place a leek half on each serving plate, cut side up, and position the razor clam shells on top. Garnish with the chickweed and apple blossom cress.

LITTLE LAYERED FENNEL POTS

Petits pots de fenouil en multi textures

Serves 6

Active time
40 minutes

Chilling time
1 hour

Cooking time
20 minutes

Equipment
Blender
Fine-mesh sieve
6 × 5–6½ fl. oz. (150–200 ml) glass jars
Mandoline

Ingredients

Parmesan cookies
1¾ oz. (50 g) freshly grated Parmesan
Scant ½ cup (1¾ oz./50 g) all-purpose flour
3 tbsp plus 1 tsp (1¾ oz./50 g) softened butter

Fennel puree
12 oz. (350 g) fennel bulbs
A little olive oil
1 star anise

Creamed fennel
1½ sheets (3 g) gold bloom gelatin
5½ oz. (160 g) fennel puree
⅓ cup (70 ml) cream, minimum 35% fat

Braised fennel
1 fennel bulb
3 tbsp (50 ml) olive oil
¾ cup (200 ml) fennel juice (homemade using a juicer)
3 tbsp (50 ml) pastis or other anise-flavored spirit
Fine sea salt and white pepper

Fennel salad
¼ fennel bulb
A few ice cubes
Squeeze of lemon juice

To serve
2 oz. (50 g) samphire
⅛ bunch dill
Olive oil for seasoning
12–18 borage flowers
Finely grated lemon zest
Salt and freshly ground pepper

PREPARING THE PARMESAN COOKIES
Knead all the ingredients together by hand to form a dough. Roll into a log 1¼ in. (4 cm) in diameter, cover in plastic wrap, and chill for about 30 minutes. Preheat the oven to 350°F (180°C/Gas mark 4) and line a baking sheet with parchment paper. Cut the log into ¾-in. (2-cm) slices, place flat on the baking sheet, and bake for about 10 minutes until golden. Let cool on a wire rack.

PREPARING THE FENNEL PUREE
Wash and slice the fennel (see technique p. 55). In a saucepan over low heat, gently cook the fennel with the olive oil and star anise until soft. Remove the star anise, blend the fennel until smooth, and then push it through a fine-mesh sieve to make a light, smooth puree. Weigh out 5½ oz. (160 g) and reserve the rest. For the next step, the weighed-out puree must be hot.

PREPARING THE CREAMED FENNEL
Soak the gelatin in a bowl of cold water until softened. Squeeze the excess water from the gelatin and stir it into the hot fennel puree until dissolved. Cool and refrigerate until just beginning to set. Before it is firm, lightly whisk the cream, and fold it into the puree. Divide the mixture between the jars, filling them to just under 1 in. (2 cm) below the rim, and return to the refrigerator to set.

PREPARING THE BRAISED FENNEL
Wash and finely slice the fennel. In a small sauté pan, sweat it over low heat with the olive oil. Pour in the fennel juice, cover with a disk of parchment paper, and continue to cook gently until tender. Season with salt and pepper, add the pastis, and keep warm.

PREPARING THE FENNEL SALAD
Wash the fennel and finely slice on a mandoline. Place in a bowl of water with a few ice cubes added and stir in the lemon juice to prevent discoloration.

TO SERVE
In a saucepan of unsalted boiling water, blanch the samphire (see technique p. 88) and refresh in a bowl of ice water. Wash and chop the dill, reserving a few sprigs for garnish. Drain the fennel for the salad, pat dry with paper towel, and season with the olive oil, salt, pepper, and dill. Divide the creamed fennel among the jars. In each jar, spoon some fennel puree over the creamed fennel. Roughly crush a Parmesan cookie and sprinkle over. Spoon the braised fennel over the crumbled cookie and add a layer of fennel salad. Top with the samphire, reserved dill sprigs, borage flowers, and the lemon zest.

PINK GARLIC CROQUETTES WITH RAMP PESTO

Cromesquis d'ail rose, pesto d'ail des ours

Serves 6

Active time
1 hour

Cooking time
30 minutes

Equipment
Fine-mesh sieve
4-in. (10-cm) round
cookie cutter, 1½ in.
(4 cm) deep
Blender
Food processor
Pot with deep-frying
basket or deep fryer
Thermometer
Mandoline

Ingredients

Pink garlic
4 heads pink garlic
3 eggs
2 oz. (50 g) garlic flower
stems (scapes)
Fleur de sel
Freshly ground pepper

Ramp pesto
1 lb. (500 g) ramps
Scant ½ cup (100 ml)
virgin olive oil

Bread-crumb coating
1 lb. (500 g) sandwich
loaf
3 eggs
1⅔ cups (7 oz./200 g)
all-purpose flour
Peanut oil for deep-
frying

To garnish and serve
2 large garlic cloves
Peanut oil for frying
1 oz. (30 g) purple garlic
flowers

PREPARING THE PINK GARLIC

Peel the garlic cloves and remove the germs. In a saucepan of boiling water, parboil them twice (see technique p. 89). Hard-boil the eggs and peel off the shells. Separate the yolks from the whites and push the whites through a fine-mesh sieve to produce a semolina-like texture. Cut the garlic cloves into brunoise (see technique p. 60) and chop or snip the garlic flower stems (see Chefs' Notes p. 54). Stir all the ingredients together and season with salt and pepper. Flatten the mixture in an even layer on a board and cut out 6 disks using the cookie cutter. Place in the freezer to firm up as this will make them easier to coat.

PREPARING THE RAMP PESTO

Set aside 6 ramp leaves to dry out for garnish. Blanch the remaining ramps in a saucepan of boiling salted water (see technique p. 88). Drain and, when cool enough to handle, squeeze out the excess water. Blend with the olive oil until smooth.

PREPARING THE BREAD-CRUMB COATING

Reduce the bread to crumbs in a food processor. Beat the eggs in a shallow dish and spread the flour and bread crumbs on separate plates. Remove the garlic disks from the freezer and dip them first into the flour, followed by the beaten egg, and lastly the bread crumbs, until coated. Repeat the procedure, pressing on the bread crumbs to give a good, even coating. Chill until ready to fry. Heat the oil for deep-frying to 320°F (160°C) and fry the croquettes until golden brown all over (see technique p. 100).

TO GARNISH AND SERVE

Dry out the 6 reserved ramp leaves in a microwave oven. Peel the garlic cloves and slice them thinly on a mandoline. Blanch the slices in a saucepan of boiling water, drain, and dry on paper towel. Fry in a little hot oil until pale golden and drain immediately on paper towel. Spoon the ramp pesto into serving bowls and place the croquettes on top. Garnish with the dried ramp leaves, purple garlic flowers, and fried garlic slices.

PANNA COTTA IN ONION SHELLS

Pannacotta en coque d'oignon

Serves 10

Active time
1 hour

Cooking time
1¼ hours

Drying time
1 hour

Resting time
10 minutes

Equipment
Immersion blender
Mandoline
Silicone baking mat
Length of stainless
steel tubing, 2 in. (5 cm)
in diameter
Fine-mesh sieve
Siphon + 2 cartridges
Pot with deep-frying
basket or deep fryer
Thermometer

Ingredients

Onion shells
4 white onions
Butter for the skillet

Onion panna cotta
3½ oz. (100 g) white
onions
Scant ½ cup (100 ml)
whole milk
¾ oz. (200 ml) cream,
minimum 35% fat
3 sheets (6 g) gelatin
Salt and white pepper

Onion chips
1 Roscoff or other sweet
onion
Confectioners' sugar
for dusting

Onion crumble
4 tbsp (20 oz./60 g)
unsalted butter,
softened
½ cup (2 oz./60 g) all-
purpose flour
¼ cup (1 oz./30 g)
almonds, chopped
2 oz. (60 g) onions,
peeled and finely
chopped
Leaves of 3 rosemary
sprigs, finely chopped

Brik pastry tubes
Clarified butter
for brushing
2 sheets brik pastry

Onion foam
9 oz. (250 g) yellow
onions
1 tbsp plus 2 tsp (25 ml)
reduced fat milk
1 tbsp (6 g) freshly
grated Parmesan
⅓ cup (75 ml) whipping
cream, minimum 35% fat

Fried pearl onion rings
6 white pearl onions
Scant ½ cup (100 ml)
whole milk
¾ cup plus 2 tbsp
(3½ oz./100 g) all-
purpose flour
Oil for frying
Fine sea salt

Pickled red onion
1 red onion
¾ cup (200 ml) water
Scant ½ cup (100 ml)
white or cider vinegar
Scant ½ cup
(2¾ oz./80 g) sugar

To serve
2 scallions
20 white and
purple garlic flowers

PREPARING THE ONION SHELLS

Preheat the oven to 325°F (160°C/Gas mark 3). Peel the onions and cut them in half lengthwise. Melt a little butter in a skillet and lightly brown the onions. Transfer to an ovenproof dish and bake for about 30 minutes. Separate the layers to make the shells and set aside.

PREPARING THE ONION PANNA COTTA

Peel and slice the onions (see technique p. 55). Place the onions, milk, and cream in a small heavy saucepan over low heat and cover with the lid. Cook gently until very soft. Soak the gelatin in a bowl of cold water until softened. Squeeze out excess water and stir the gelatin into the hot onion mixture until melted. Process with an immersion blender and season with salt and pepper. Let cool, pour into the onion shells, and let set.

PREPARING THE ONION CHIPS

Preheat the oven to 175°F (80°C/Gas at lowest possible setting) on conventional heat. Peel the onion and, using a mandoline, cut it vertically into fine slices. Carefully place each slice flat on a silicone baking mat and dust with confectioners' sugar. Let the onion slices rest for 10 minutes, then dry them out in the oven for 1 hour.

PREPARING THE ONION CRUMBLE

Preheat the oven to 325°F (160°C/Gas mark 3). Rub all the ingredients together with your fingertips until you obtain coarse crumbs. Sprinkle over a silicone baking mat and bake for about 10 minutes, until very pale golden.

PREPARING THE BRIK PASTRY TUBES

To make the clarified butter, melt the butter gently over low heat in a heavy saucepan. Skim off the froth, then pour the clear yellow layer of clarified butter into a jug, leaving behind the milky residue. Preheat the oven to 350°F (180°C/Gas mark 4). Cut the sheets of brik pastry into 2-×10-in. (5-×25-cm) rectangles and brush them with the clarified butter. Roll the rectangles around the stainless steel tubing, holding them in place with aluminum foil, and bake in the oven for 8 minutes. Bake in batches, if necessary. Carefully remove from the tube while still hot and reserve at room temperature.

PREPARING THE ONION FOAM

Peel and slice the onions (see technique p. 55). Place in a saucepan half-filled with water, cover, and cook over low heat until very soft. Drain the onions, process with an immersion blender, and strain through a fine-mesh sieve. Warm the milk and stir in the Parmesan. Add to the onions along with the cream, season with salt and pepper, and transfer to a siphon. Fit with two cartridges and refrigerate.

PREPARING THE FRIED PEARL ONION RINGS

Heat an oil bath to 340°F (170°C). Peel the onions and slice them into rings. Dip in the milk and then in the flour until coated. Fry the rings until lightly colored. Drain on paper towel and season with salt.

PREPARING THE PICKLED RED ONION

Peel and cut the onion in half lengthwise, and then cut into slices, again lengthwise, just under ½ in. (1 cm) thick. In a medium saucepan over high heat, bring the water, vinegar, and sugar to a boil. Remove from the heat, add the onion slices, and let cool to room temperature.

TO SERVE

Finely slice the scallion greens. Garnish the panna cotta-filled onion shells with the sliced scallion greens, fried onion rings, and garlic flowers. Place 3 filled onion shells on each serving plate. Pipe a little onion foam into each brik pastry tube and stand upright on the plates. Arrange a little crumble, some pickled red onion, and an onion chip on each plate.

SHALLOTS STUFFED WITH LAMB AND CREAMED GRAY SHALLOTS

Échalotes farcies à l'agneau et crème d'échalote grise

Serves 6

Active time
1 hour

Cooking time
50 minutes

Equipment
Meat grinder
Steam oven or steamer
Blender

Ingredients

Shallots
6 banana shallots (cuisse de poulet shallots)

Lamb stuffing
6 tbsp (3 oz./90 g) unsalted butter
1 tsp (5 g) golden raisins
9 oz. (250 g) lamb shoulder
2½ oz. (70 g) pork collar or neck fillet
2½ oz. (75 g) shallots
1 tbsp olive oil
⅔ cup (150 ml) dry white wine
¼ bunch flat-leaf parsley
¼ bunch mint
¼ bunch chives
1 tsp chopped fresh oregano
4 piquillo peppers
Salt and freshly ground pepper

Creamed gray shallots
10 oz. (300 g) gray shallots
3 tbsp (2 oz./50 g) butter
¾ cup (200 ml) vegetable stock, plus a little extra if necessary
3 tbsp (50 ml) whipping cream, minimum 35% fat
Salt and freshly ground pepper

To garnish and serve
Green parts of 6 scallions
Scant ½ cup (100 ml) lamb *jus*
Purple garlic flowers

PREPARING THE SHALLOTS
Preheat the oven to 350°F (180°C/Gas mark 4). Place the shallots in a tightly sealed parchment paper package and bake for 25 minutes. Unwrap, separate the shallot layers and set aside the largest ones for serving.

PREPARING THE LAMB STUFFING
Clarify the butter by melting it gently over low heat in a heavy saucepan. Skim off the froth, then pour the clear yellow layer of clarified butter into a jug, leaving behind the milky residue. You will need about 4 tablespoons (60 ml) for the stuffing. Soak the golden raisins in a little warm water. In a meat grinder, grind the lamb shoulder and pork collar or fillet. Peel and chop the shallots into brunoise (see technique p. 60) and then sauté lightly in a skillet with the olive oil, without letting them color. Deglaze with the white wine and cook until the wine has completely evaporated. Transfer to a bowl and let cool. Chop the parsley and mint (see technique p. 54). Wash and chop or snip the chives (see Chefs' Notes p. 54). Stir all the herbs into the cooked shallot. Return to the skillet and sweat the mixture briefly. Stir the mixture into the ground meat and season with salt and pepper. Drain the raisins. Finely dice the piquillo peppers and stir them into the mixture with the raisins. Using two large spoons, shape the stuffing into generous ovals. Wrap each one in a shallot layer. Brush with clarified butter and cook in a steam oven at 185°F (85°C) or a steamer for 10 minutes.

PREPARING THE CREAMED GRAY SHALLOTS
Chop the shallots (see technique p. 56). Melt the butter in a large skillet and sweat them without letting them color. Pour in the vegetable stock, cover with the lid, and simmer over low heat for about 15 minutes. Blend until smooth and pour in the cream. If you need to thin the mixture a little, stir in a little more vegetable stock. Season with salt and pepper.

TO SERVE
Blanch the green parts of the scallions, drain, and refresh (see technique p. 88). Serve on individual serving plates or on 2 plates to share. Outline an uneven circle with the creamed gray shallots and pour a little lamb *jus* in the center. Arrange the scallion greens and stuffed shallots on the plate in the form of flowers and garnish with purple garlic flowers.

BLOODY MARY-STYLE CELERY

Céleri Bloody Mary

Serves 6

Active time
2 hours

Chilling time
2 hours

Cooking time
35 minutes

Equipment
Juicer
Blender
Coffee filter
Fine-mesh sieve
Silicone baking mat
with a leaf pattern
4-in. (10-cm) tart ring,
¾ in. (2 cm) deep

Ingredients

**Gelled celery
and celery sticks**
5 sheets (10 g) gold
bloom gelatin
2 bunches celery stalks
2 cups (500 ml) still
mineral water
½ tsp (1 g) agar agar
Salt and freshly ground
pepper

Gelled Bloody Mary
6 sheets (12 g) gold
bloom gelatin
4 tomatoes
2 tsp (10 g) tomato
ketchup
2 tsp (10 g) tomato paste
¾ cup (200 ml) vodka,
plus more for serving
2 tsp (10 ml) Tabasco
sauce, plus more
for serving
Celery salt
2 tsp (10 ml)
Worcestershire sauce

Lacy tomato tuiles
½ cup minus 1 tbsp
(2 oz./50 g) all-purpose
flour
3 tbsp plus 1 tsp
(2 oz./50 g) melted
butter
Scant ¼ cup (2 oz./50 g)
egg white (about
2 whites)
1 tsp (5 g) tomato paste

To garnish and serve
30 coriander seeds
4 tsp (20 ml) virgin
olive oil
Celery salt
Yellow celery leaves
Smoked paprika

PREPARING THE GELLED CELERY AND CELERY STICKS

Soak the gelatin in a bowl of cold water until softened. Wash and peel the celery stalks, reserving all the peel for the jelly. Cut 1 bunch of stalks into small matchsticks and cook *à l'anglaise* in a saucepan of boiling salted water (see technique p. 90). Refresh in cold water, drain, season with salt and pepper, and set aside. Juice the other bunch of celery stalks with the peel. Stir in the mineral water, strain, and pour the juice into a saucepan. Add the agar agar and bring to a boil. Remove from the heat. Squeeze the excess water from the gelatin and stir in until completely dissolved. Pour into a rimmed baking sheet or large dish. Let set in the refrigerator for 1 hour and then cut into small cubes.

PREPARING THE GELLED BLOODY MARY

Soak the gelatin in a bowl of cold water until softened. Wash and hull the tomatoes. Blend them with the ketchup, tomato paste, vodka, and Tabasco sauce. Heat the mixture in a saucepan, then fit a coffee filter in a fine-mesh sieve and strain the mixture, pressing down well. Reserve the remaining pulp. Squeeze the excess water from the gelatin and stir it into the strained liquid, reheated if necessary, until dissolved. Pour into a rimmed baking sheet or large dish. Let set in the refrigerator for 1 hour and then cut into small cubes. Season the remaining pulp like a Bloody Mary, with a little vodka, celery salt, and Tabasco and Worcestershire sauces.

PREPARING THE LACY TOMATO TUILES

Preheat the oven to 320°F (160°C/Gas mark 3). Place the silicone baking mat with a leaf pattern on a baking sheet. In a medium bowl, whisk all the ingredients together. Spread the batter evenly over the baking mat and bake for 4–5 minutes. Let firm up and, when cool enough to handle, remove the tuiles from the mat.

TO SERVE

Place the 4-in. (10-cm) tart ring on a serving plate and spoon some of the reserved pulp from preparing the gelled Bloody Mary into the ring. Season the celery sticks with the coriander seeds, olive oil, and celery salt and arrange them on the pulp with a lacy tomato tuile. Add more celery sticks and finish with another lacy tuile. Carefully remove the ring and repeat with the other serving plates. Arrange the two types of cubed jelly alternately around the edge, decorate with yellow celery leaves, and sprinkle with smoked paprika.

ROOT AND TUBER VEGETABLES

CARROT CAKE

Cake à la carotte

Serves 6

Active time
1½ hours

Chilling time
1½–2 hours

Freezing time
3 hours minimum

Cooking time
15 minutes

Equipment
Juicer
Ice-cream maker
8-in. (20-cm) square cake frame, ¾ in. (2 cm) deep, or brownie pan
Electric hand beater
2½-in. (6-cm) round cookie cutter
Mandoline
100 ml pipette or squeeze bottle
Stand mixer
Pastry bag

Ingredients

Carrot, orange, and apricot sorbet
1 lb. 6 oz. (620 g) carrots
¼ cup (60 ml) lemon juice
1½ cups (345 ml) orange juice
3½ oz. (100 g) apricot puree
Generous ⅔ cup (4½ oz./130 g) granulated sugar
⅕ oz. (6 g) stabilizer (optional)

Carrot cake
⅔ cup plus 1 tbsp (3 oz./90 g) all-purpose flour
1 tbsp plus ½ tsp (13 g) baking powder
11 oz. (320 g) carrots

½ cup (4½ oz./130 g) lightly beaten egg (about 2½ eggs)
⅔ cup (4½ oz./130 g) granulated sugar
1 pinch of fleur de sel
¼ cup (2 oz./60 g) egg white (about 2 whites)
2¼ cups (6¾ oz./190 g) ground hazelnuts
4 tsp (20 ml) grapeseed oil
Scant ½ cup (100 ml) hazelnut oil
⅔ cup (2¾ oz./75 g) chopped toasted hazelnuts

Candied carrots and syrup
1 purple carrot
1 orange carrot
1 white carrot
1⅔ cups (11½ oz./325 g) sugar
1½ cups (325 ml) water

Carrot jelly
1¾ sheets (3.5 g) gelatin
1⅔ cups (400 ml) carrot juice
½ cup (3½ oz./100 g) sugar
1¾ tsp (2.5 g) agar agar

Apricot coulis
2½ tsp (8 g) cornstarch
10 oz. (300 g) apricot puree
5 tsp (¾ oz./20 g) sugar

Mascarpone whipped cream
⅓ cup (75 g) mascarpone
1¼ cups (300 ml) cream, minimum 35% fat
¼ cup (2 oz./50 g) sugar
Seeds of 1 vanilla bean

To serve
18 pansy petals
18–24 garlic flowers
Carrot fronds

PREPARING THE CARROT, ORANGE, AND APRICOT SORBET

Peel and juice the carrots. In a large saucepan, combine the carrot juice with the lemon juice, orange juice, and apricot puree and warm slightly. Stir in the sugar and stabilizer, if using, and chill for 1 hour. Churn in an ice-cream maker according to the manufacturer's instructions and freeze for at least 3 hours.

PREPARING THE CARROT CAKE

Preheat the oven to 325°F (170°C/Gas mark 3). Place the cake frame on a baking sheet lined with parchment paper. Sift the flour with the baking powder into a mixing bowl. Peel and grate the carrots. Using an electric hand beater, whisk the eggs with the sugar for 5 minutes to the ribbon stage, and then whisk in the fleur de sel. Whisk the egg whites until they hold soft peaks and set aside. Stir the ground hazelnuts, grapeseed oil, hazelnut oil, grated carrots, and hazelnuts into the whisked eggs and sugar. Lightly fold in the egg whites until incorporated. Pour the batter into the cake frame—it should be just under ½ in. (1 cm) deep. Bake for about 15 minutes, until a toothpick pushed into the center comes out clean. Transfer to a wire rack, lift off the cake frame, and let cool to room temperature. Using the cookie cutter, cut out 6 disks.

PREPARING THE CANDIED CARROTS

Wash and peel the carrots. Using the mandoline, finely slice them, keeping the different colors separate. In a large saucepan over medium-high heat, dissolve the sugar in the water and bring to a boil to make a syrup. Divide the syrup equally among 3 small saucepans (about ¾ cup/200 ml in each). Over low heat, cook each color of carrot separately in the syrup until candied. Let cool.

PREPARING THE CARROT JELLY

Soak the gelatin in a bowl of cold water until softened. In a small saucepan, bring the carrot juice, sugar, and agar agar to a boil, then remove from the heat. Squeeze the excess water from the gelatin and stir into the mixture until dissolved. Pour onto a rimmed baking sheet in a thin layer, let cool, and chill until set. Using the cookie cutter, cut out 6 disks.

PREPARING THE APRICOT COULIS

Stir the cornstarch into 2 tablespoons of cold water until smooth. In a small saucepan, heat the apricot puree and stir in the sugar and diluted cornstarch. Bring to a boil, stirring constantly, until thickened to the desired consistency. Let cool, then transfer to the pipette or squeeze bottle.

PREPARING THE MASCARPONE WHIPPED CREAM

In the bowl of a stand mixer fitted with the whisk, beat the mascarpone, cream, sugar, and vanilla seeds until the mixture holds soft peaks. Chill and then transfer to a pastry bag.

TO ASSEMBLE AND SERVE

Place a disk of carrot jelly on each disk of carrot cake. Snip off the tip of the pastry bag and pipe small mounds of mascarpone cream on top. Carefully arrange the candied carrot slices over the cream and garnish with the pansy petals and garlic flowers. Serve a large quenelle of sorbet on the side and place some carrot fronds at one end to form a "carrot." Pipe small dots of apricot coulis onto each plate.

HAY-INFUSED POTATO CARBONARA

Pomme de terre à la carbonara au foin

Serves 10

Active time
1 hour

Marinating time
1 hour

Cooking time
1 hour

Equipment
Spiralizer
Carving fork
Perforated baking sheet
Steam oven or steamer

Ingredients

Marinated eggs
10 egg yolks
Sufficient soy sauce to cover the yolks

Potato nests
5 large floury potatoes, such as Agria

Onions
2 tsp (10 g) butter
10 large white onion bottoms (root end)
2½ tsp (10 g) sugar
1 pinch salt

Smoked tofu sticks
7 oz. (200 g) smoked tofu

Hay-infused cream
2½ cups (600 ml) cream, minimum 35% fat
1 handful food-grade hay

To serve
7 oz. (200 g) freshly grated Parmesan
Snipped chives
Freshly ground pepper

PREPARING THE MARINATED EGGS
One hour before serving, place the egg yolks in a dish, spoon over enough soy sauce to cover them, and leave to marinate in the refrigerator until serving.

PREPARING THE POTATO NESTS
Peel the potatoes and pass them through a spiralizer to produce spaghetti-like strings. Rinse well and reserve in a large bowl of cold water, ready to steam just before serving.

PREPARING THE ONIONS
Melt the butter in a saucepan, add the onion bottoms, cover the pan, and sweat until softened. Pour in sufficient water to cover them, stir in the sugar and salt, and cook uncovered until the liquid has reduced and the onion bottoms are glazed and very tender.

PREPARING THE SMOKED TOFU STICKS
Cut the smoked tofu into matchsticks. Sauté in a skillet without any added fat, over medium-high heat until crisp.

PREPARING THE HAY-INFUSED CREAM
In a saucepan over medium heat, warm the cream with the hay, and then simmer gently until the cream is reduced by half. Strain and keep warm.

TO ASSEMBLE AND SERVE
Just before serving, drain the potato "spaghetti" and, using a carving fork, shape it into 10 small nests. Place on a perforated baking sheet and cook in a steam oven or steamer for 3-4 minutes, or until just al dente. Place a glazed onion bottom in the center of each serving plate and pour over a generous serving of the infused cream. Position the potato nests on top, then carefully lift the egg yolks out of the marinade and place on top of the nests. Scatter the tofu matchsticks around. Season with freshly ground pepper and sprinkle liberally with grated Parmesan and snipped chives.

POTATO CHARTREUSE, BLACK MULLET TARTARE, AND SHISO TEMPURA

Chartreuse de pommes de terre, tartare de mulet noir et tempura de shiso

Serves 6

Active time
45 minutes

Cooking time
20 minutes

Equipment
Apple corer
Skimmer
Siphon + 2 cartridges
Pot with deep-frying basket or deep fryer
2½-in. (6-cm) round cookie cutter

Ingredients

Potatoes
2¼ lb. (1 kg) waxy potatoes
4 cups (1 liter) shellfish stock
A few saffron threads

Black mullet tartare
1 lb. (500 g) black mullet fillets
1 oz. (30 g) fresh ginger
½ bunch chives
1 green shiso leaf
7 mertensia (oyster plant) leaves
1 oz. (30 g) miso paste
2 tsp (10 ml) yuzu juice
2 tsp (10 ml) sake

Yogurt and yuzu foam
2½ sheets (3 g) gelatin
Scant ¼ cup (50 ml) milk
1½ cups (350 g) plain yogurt
Scant ½ cup (100 ml) cream, minimum 35% fat
4 tsp (20 ml) yuzu juice
Fine sea salt

Shiso tempura
¾ cup (200 ml) sparkling water
1 egg yolk
¾ cup plus 3 tbsp (3½ oz./110 g) all-purpose flour
6 large shiso leaves
Generous ⅓ cup (2 oz./60 g) cornstarch
Peanut oil for frying
Fine sea salt

To assemble and serve
6 long chive stems
6 borage flowers
Shichimi togarashi (Japanese seven-spice mix)

PREPARING THE POTATOES
Wash and peel the potatoes. Using an apple corer, cut them into cylinders. Pour the shellfish stock into a large saucepan over low heat and add the saffron. Cook the cylinders for about 10 minutes, until tender when pierced with the tip of a knife, remove from the saucepan with a skimmer, and let cool.

PREPARING THE BLACK MULLET TARTARE
Cut the fillets into small, even dice. Peel and grate the ginger and wash and chop or snip the chives (see Chefs' Notes p. 54). Wash and chop the shiso and mertensia leaves. Combine the miso paste, ginger, chives, shiso leaf, mertensia leaves, yuzu juice, and sake and mix with the diced mullet. Refrigerate until serving.

PREPARING THE YOGURT AND YUZU FOAM
Soak the gelatin in a bowl of cold water until softened. In a saucepan, warm the milk over medium heat, stir in the yogurt, cream, and yuzu juice, and season with salt. When the mixture is hot but not boiling, remove from the heat. Squeeze the excess water from the gelatin and stir it in until completely dissolved. Pour the mixture into the siphon, fit it with the cartridges, and refrigerate until serving.

PREPARING THE SHISO TEMPURA
Beat together the water, egg yolk, and flour. Dip the shiso leaves in the cornstarch to absorb any moisture, so the batter sticks to them better, and then in the tempura batter until coated. Heat an oil bath to 350°F (180°C) and fry the shiso leaves for a few minutes, until golden and crisp. Drain on paper towel, season with salt, and keep warm.

TO ASSEMBLE AND SERVE
Place the cookie cutter on a serving plate and create a ring of potato cylinders by standing them inside the cutter to line the edge. Spoon a portion of mullet tartare into the center, carefully remove the cutter, tie a chive stem around to hold the potato cylinders in place, and top with a borage flower. Repeat with the remaining ingredients to make five more servings. Place a leaf of shiso tempura on each plate. Using the siphon, pipe out a small amount of the yogurt and yuzu foam and sprinkle with a little shichimi togarashi.

POTATO AND MUSHROOM GRATIN WITH MORBIER CHEESE

Gratin de pommes de terre et champignons au morbier

Serves 6

Active time
30 minutes

Cooking time
1½ hours

Equipment
Mandoline
Large baking dish
Skimmer

Ingredients
4½ lb. (2 kg) waxy potatoes
2 garlic cloves
7 tbsp (3½ oz./100 g) butter, divided
10 oz. (300 g) button mushrooms
14 oz. (400 g) Morbier cheese (or another semi-soft cow's milk cheese, such as Swiss Raclette, Vacherin Fribourgeois, or Italian Fontina)
1¼ cups (300 ml) reduced fat milk
3¼ cups (800 ml) cream, minimum 35% fat
Freshly grated nutmeg
Fine sea salt and freshly ground pepper

PREPARING THE GRATIN

Wash and peel the potatoes and slice them finely on the mandoline. Do not wash them after slicing.

Peel and chop the garlic (see technique p. 56). Rub the baking dish with 3 tablespoons (50 g) of the butter and spread the chopped garlic over the base.

Clean the mushrooms (see technique p. 35) and slice them. In a skillet, melt the remaining butter, sauté the mushrooms, and season with salt and pepper. Drain them from the skillet using a skimmer.

Preheat the oven to 325°F (160°C/Gas mark 3). Layer the mushroom and potato slices alternately in the ovenproof dish, seasoning with salt and pepper between each layer. Cut the cheese into small cubes. Combine the milk with the cream in a mixing bowl and stir in the nutmeg. Pour the mixture over the potatoes and mushrooms, scatter the cheese cubes over the top, and bake for 1½ hours, or until tender when the tip of a knife is pushed into the center through the layers.

The gratin must be very tender, the cream and milk mixture well reduced, and the top a beautiful golden brown.

CHEFS' NOTES

Morbier cheese originates from the village of Morbier in the east of France. It is immediately recognizable by the distinctive black line that runs through the middle of it. This was originally ash but is now usually a vegetable dye.

CREAMY MASHED POTATOES WITH SCALLIONS AND PARSLEY

Pomme purée à la cive et persil plat

Serves 6

Active time
20 minutes

Cooking time
30 minutes

Equipment
Skimmer
Food mill

Ingredients
4½ lb. (2 kg) floury potatoes
1¼ cups (300 ml) reduced fat milk
1¾ sticks (7 oz./200 g) butter, diced
1⅔ cups (400 ml) cream, minimum 35% fat
Nutmeg
Coarse sea salt
Fine sea salt and freshly ground pepper

To serve
1 bunch flat-leaf parsley, washed and chopped
1 bunch scallions or spring onions, trimmed and sliced
Olive oil infused with herbs of your choice

PREPARING THE MASHED POTATOES

Wash and peel the potatoes and cut each one in half. Place in a large saucepan and pour in enough cold water to cover them. Add a good pinch of coarse sea salt, bring to a boil over high heat, and skim any starch from the surface. Reduce the heat and simmer, until tender when pierced with the tip of a knife. Warm the milk. Drain the potatoes and let them dry briefly in their steam. While they are still hot, pass the potatoes through a food mill. Mix in the diced butter with a spatula, followed by the cream and warmed milk. Grate in a little nutmeg and season with salt and pepper.

TO SERVE

Spoon the mashed potatoes into an attractive serving dish and scatter with the chopped parsley and sliced scallions or spring onions. Drizzle over a few drops of herb-infused olive oil.

CHEFS' NOTES

If you cut the potatoes into small chunks, you risk them absorbing too much water and they will have an elastic texture when mashed.

PONT-NEUF POTATOES WITH PIQUILLO KETCHUP

Pommes Pont-Neuf, ketchup piquillos

Serves 6

Active time
25 minutes

Cooking time
40 minutes

Equipment
Blender
Skimmer
Large pot with deep-frying basket or deep fryer
Thermometer

Ingredients

Piquillo ketchup
1 garlic clove
1 oz. (30 g) fresh ginger
1 cup (7 oz./200 g) brown sugar
1 cup (250 ml) Banyuls vinegar
1 lb. (500 g) canned piquillo peppers, well drained

Pont-Neuf potatoes
4½ lb. (2 kg) all-round potatoes, such as Yukon Gold
8½ cups (2 liters) oil for frying
Fleur de sel
Piment d'Espelette

PREPARING THE PIQUILLO KETCHUP
Peel the garlic clove, remove the germ, and chop. Peel and grate the ginger. In a sauté pan over low heat, slowly melt the sugar and then simmer with the vinegar to make a sweet-and-savory sauce. Stir in the garlic and ginger, add the piquillo peppers, and simmer gently for about 30 minutes. Transfer to a blender and process until smooth. Season to taste, depending on whether you prefer the sauce to be spicy or sweet.

PREPARING THE PONT-NEUF POTATOES
Wash and peel the potatoes. Cut them into large fries about ¾ in. (1.5 cm) wide and 2¾ in. (7 cm) long. Bring a large saucepan of water to a boil and blanch the potatoes, skimming any starchy foam from the surface. Drain and dry thoroughly with paper towel. Heat the oil in a fryer to 350°F (180°C) and deep-fry the potatoes until a rich golden brown. Drain on paper towel and season with fleur de sel and piment d'Espelette.

TO SERVE
Serve the Pont-Neuf potatoes in parchment paper cones with the piquillo ketchup in a bowl for dipping.

CHEFS' NOTES

The ketchup will keep for several days in a sealed container in the refrigerator.

LAYERED SWEET POTATO AND POTATO CAKE

Patates douces façon pommes moulées

Serves 6

Active time
1½ hours

Cooking time
1 hour

Equipment
Skimmer
Mandoline
2¾-in. (7-cm) plain round cookie cutter
1¾-in. (4-cm) plain round cookie cutter
2 × 6-in. (15-cm) charlotte molds (see Chefs' Notes)

Ingredients

Clarified butter
1 stick plus 2 tbsp (5 oz./150 g) lightly salted butter

Potatoes
5 lb. (2.5 kg) waxy potatoes, such as Charlotte
2 large orange sweet potatoes
9 oz. (250 g) tomme or other semi-hard cheese
Salt and freshly ground pepper

PREPARING THE CLARIFIED BUTTER

In a heavy saucepan, melt the butter gently over low heat. Skim off the froth, then pour the clear yellow layer of clarified butter into a jug, leaving behind the milky residue.

PREPARING THE POTATOES

Wash and peel the potatoes and sweet potatoes. Using the mandoline, cut both into ¼-in. (5-mm) thick slices. Using the 2¾-in (7-cm) cutter, cut out a disk of sweet potato for the top layer of the potato cake. Using the 1¾-in. (4-cm) cutter, cut the remaining slices of both types of potato into disks. Blanch the potato and sweet potato slices in separate saucepans of unsalted boiling water for 2–3 minutes, to release some of the starch and make assembling the layers easier. Drain without refreshing.

TO ASSEMBLE AND SERVE

Preheat the oven to 475°F (250°C/Gas mark 9) and place a baking sheet in the oven to heat. Brush one of the charlotte molds with clarified butter. Place the larger sweet potato disk on the bottom of the mold, in the center, then arrange a ring of overlapping sweet potato disks over the rest of the bottom. Grate some of the cheese into the center. Continue, adding alternate layers of potato and sweet potato disks, overlapping them in rings and changing the direction of the disks each time. Press down firmly on each layer with the base of the second charlotte mold before adding the next. Brush each layer with clarified butter, season generously, and grate more cheese into the center each time. Place the filled mold in the oven on the hot baking sheet, reduce the temperature to 450°F (230°C/Gas mark 8), and bake for 5 minutes. Reduce the temperature to 400°F (200°C/Gas mark 6) and bake for 20 minutes, until sufficiently colored on top. Cover with a sheet of aluminum foil and bake for an additional 20 minutes. Let rest for a few minutes so the temperature is even throughout the layers, before carefully unmolding onto a serving dish.

CHEFS' NOTES

One charlotte mold is needed to bake the cake; the other is used to press down on the slices as you build up the layers. If you do not have a second mold, a flat plate the same size as the diameter of the charlotte mold can be used instead.

ANISE-SCENTED WHITE TURNIP RAVIOLI AND SLOW-COOKED COD

Ravioles de navet blanc à l'anis et cabillaud confit à l'huile d'olive

Serves 10

Active time
1½ hours

Marinating time
12 hours

Cooking time
1 hour

Equipment
Fine-mesh sieve
Instant-read thermometer
Electric hand whisk
Mandoline
Cookie cutter suitable for the size of the turnips
Immersion blender
Steam oven or steamer
Small flower-shaped cutters

Ingredients

Lemon condiment
10 lemons
2½ tsp (10 g) kosher salt
1 cup plus 2 tbsp (7¾ oz./220 g) granulated sugar

Slow-cooked cod
6 cups (1.5 liters) olive oil
10 cod steaks with skin on

Black currant butter
3½ oz. (100 g) black currant puree (or use blueberry puree)
7 tbsp (3½ oz./100 g) softened butter

Ravioli
2 lb. 10 oz. (1.2 kg) long white turnips
Scant ½ cup (100 ml) cream, minimum 35% fat
1⅔ cups (400 ml) reduced fat milk
4 tbsp (2 oz./60 g) butter
A little ground aniseed

To garnish and serve
6 red meat radishes
1¼ tsp (5 g) granulated sugar
2 tsp (10 g) unsalted butter
1 pinch of fine sea salt
50 black currants (or blueberries)

PREPARING THE LEMON CONDIMENT
Cut one of the lemons into very thin slices. Place the slices in a shallow dish, sprinkle with the salt, and let marinate for 12 hours in the refrigerator. Peel the remaining lemons, removing all the white pith, and cut into thick slices. Place in a saucepan, add the sugar, and cook over low heat until the sugar dissolves. Increase the heat to medium and simmer for 20 minutes. Drain, push the pulp through a fine-mesh sieve, and let cool. Rinse the salted lemon slices, chop them finely, and stir into the strained lemon pulp. Set aside.

PREPARING THE SLOW-COOKED COD
Preheat the oven to 175°F (80°C/Gas at lowest possible setting). Pour the olive oil into an ovenproof dish and place in the oven for 20 minutes. Rinse the cod fillets, pat them dry with paper towel, and place in a single layer in the dish in the oven, making sure they are covered with oil. Push the probe of the thermometer into one of the cod fillets and cook until the core temperature reaches 124°F (51°C). Drain the fillets well and set aside, keeping them warm.

PREPARING THE BLACK CURRANT BUTTER
Whisk the black currant (or blueberry) puree with the softened butter until very smooth. Place the mixture between two sheets of parchment paper, roll out to a thickness of between 1/16–1/8 in. (2–3 mm), and place flat in the freezer.

PREPARING THE RAVIOLI
Peel the white turnips and, using the mandoline, cut into 60 very thin slices, reserving any trimmings. Trim the slices into perfect disks using the cookie cutter, again reserving the trimmings. Cook the trimmings in a saucepan with the cream, milk, butter, and aniseed until tender, and then process with an immersion blender to make a firm mousseline. Dry out in a saucepan over low heat for a few minutes, stirring vigorously with a wooden spoon, to remove excess moisture. Cook the turnip disks for about 1 minute in a steam oven at 212°F (100°C) or a steamer until just tender (see technique p. 92). Spoon a little mousseline onto each turnip disk, fold up the sides to enclose the mousseline, and pinch the edges together to seal.

TO GARNISH AND SERVE
Using an apple corer, cut the red meat radishes into 60 small cylinders. Place the radish cylinders in a saucepan and pour in enough water to half-cover them. Add the sugar, butter, and salt, and cook gently over low heat to reduce, until the radishes are glazed. Cut out flower shapes in the frozen black currant butter using the cutter, arrange a few on each serving plate, and let come to room temperature. On each plate, place a cod fillet, skin side up, and arrange 6 radish cylinders, each topped with a turnip ravioli. Scatter over a few black currants (or blueberries) and serve with the lemon condiment.

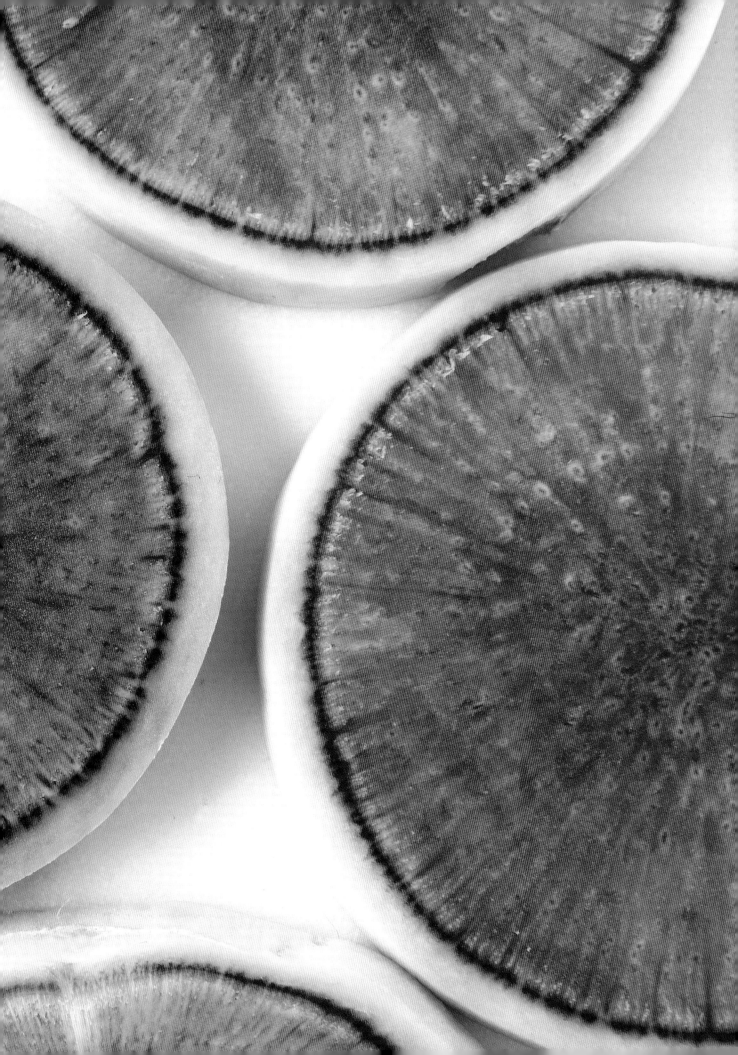

PINK RADISHES WITH SEA SALT AND RADISH LEAF BUTTER

Radis rose, croque-au-sel et beurre de fanes

Serves 6

Active time
25 minutes

Cooking time
5 minutes

Chilling time
Several hours (optional)

Equipment
Immersion blender
Pastry bag with a shell piping tip

Ingredients

Pink radishes
3 bunches pink radishes
2½ tsp (10 g) coarse sea salt

Radish leaf butter
1 stick plus 2 tbsp (5 oz./150 g) unsalted butter, diced, at room temperature
Fleur de sel
Freshly ground pepper

PREPARING THE PINK RADISHES
Remove the leaves from the radishes and trim the roots. Wash both the leaves and radishes in cold water and set aside. For a more decorative version, cut vertical slits in the radishes and place them in a bowl of ice water. Chill for several hours until they open out like flowers.

PREPARING THE RADISH LEAF BUTTER
Boil the radish leaves à *l'anglaise* (see technique p. 90). Drain, refresh, and squeeze the leaves to remove excess water. Soften the butter, blend it with the cooled leaves until smooth, and season with fleur de sel and freshly ground pepper. Spoon the butter into a pastry bag fitted with a shell tip and chill until the butter is firm enough to pipe.

TO SERVE
Pipe the radish leaf butter into shell shapes in a serving dish. Put some fleur de sel in a small bowl to serve separately. Drain the radishes and serve on small napkins or on a serving plate, to be dipped in the salt and then the radish leaf butter before eating.

RAINBOW PICKLED RADISHES

Pickles de radis multicolores

Serves 6

Active time
45 minutes

Cooking time
10 minutes

Maturing time
3 days

Equipment
1-quart (1 liter) canning jar, sterilized

Ingredients

Radishes
2 bunches multicolored radishes

Brine
2 oz. (50 g) fresh ginger
5 garlic cloves
2 cups (500 ml) cider vinegar
¾ cup (5 oz./150 g) granulated sugar
2 tbsp (10 g) coriander seeds
1 tbsp (10 g) black peppercorns
6 cloves
2 bay leaves
Sprigs of ¼ bunch fresh thyme
2 tsp (5 g) juniper berries
1½ tsp (5 g) cumin seeds

PREPARING THE RADISHES
Trim the tops of the radishes, cut off the roots, and wash. Cut them in half lengthwise and place in the jar without packing them together too tightly.

PREPARING THE BRINE
Peel and chop the ginger. Peel the garlic, leaving the cloves whole. Pour the cider vinegar into a saucepan, add the sugar, coriander seeds, peppercorns, cloves, bay leaves, thyme sprigs, ginger, juniper berries, garlic cloves, and cumin seeds, and bring slowly to a boil, stirring occasionally, until the sugar dissolves. Boil for 5 minutes, remove from the heat, and let cool.

BOTTLING THE PICKLES
Pour the cooled brine into the jar to fill it, so the radishes are covered. Close and turn upside down to remove the air. Leave to mature for at least 3 days before serving.

CHEFS' NOTES

These pickles make a good accompaniment to charcuterie and smoked foods.

CELERY ROOT TAGLIATELLE AND SLOW-COOKED VEAL

Tagliatelles de céleri et son jarret de veau

Serves 10

Active time
1 hour

Marinating time
Overnight

Cooking time
1¾–2 hours

Equipment
Nutcracker
Pestle and mortar
Spiralizer
Carving fork

Ingredients

Veal shanks
2 veal shanks
2 oz. (50 g) browned butter
6 thyme flowers
3 tbsp (50 ml) truffle *jus*
2 cups (500 ml) veal *jus*

Truffle-walnut condiment
20 walnuts
2 tbsp (30 ml) truffle *jus*
¼ cup (60 ml) grapeseed oil
1 tsp (5 ml) aged red wine vinegar
Salt and freshly ground pepper

Celery root tagliatelle and sauce
1 celery root
Juice of ½ lemon
1²⁄₃ cups (400 ml) cream, minimum 35% fat
1 oz. (30 g) freshly grated Parmesan
¾ oz. (20 g) black truffle breakings

To serve
1 bunch chives
1 oz. (30 g) freshly grated Parmesan
A few black truffle shavings (optional)
3½ oz. (100 g) fried croutons

PREPARING THE VEAL SHANKS
The day before, put the shanks in a bowl with the other ingredients and let marinate overnight. The next day, preheat the oven to 325°F (160°C/ Gas mark 3). Transfer the shanks and their marinade to an aluminum foil package, folding the edges over to make a tight seal, and cook in the oven for 1½ hours. Keep the shanks warm in the sealed package.

PREPARING THE TRUFFLE-WALNUT CONDIMENT
Shell the walnuts and pound the kernels to a paste with the truffle *jus* using a pestle and mortar. Whisk in the oil, add the vinegar, and season with salt and pepper.

PREPARING THE CELERY ROOT TAGLIATELLE AND SAUCE
Peel the celery and spiralize into tagliatelle-like ribbons. Reserve them in a bowl of water with the lemon juice added to prevent them discoloring. In a large saucepan over medium heat, cook the cream until it has reduced by about a third. Stir in the Parmesan and truffle breakings. Steam the celery root tagliatelle in a steam oven at 210°F (100°C) or steamer for 4 minutes. Add to the saucepan and stir into the cream sauce. Using the carving fork, shape the tagliatelle into nests and keep warm.

TO SERVE
Wash and chop or snip the chives (see Chefs' Notes p. 54). Place a piece of veal shank on each serving plate with a nest of celery root tagliatelle. Sprinkle the tagliatelle with grated Parmesan and chopped chives. Add some truffle shavings, if using, and fried croutons, and accompany with the truffle-walnut condiment and a little of the veal marinade.

PARSNIP CRÈME BRÛLÉE

Crème brûlée aux panais

Serves 6

Active time
1 hour

Freezing time
1 hour

Cooking time
1½ hours

Equipment
Silicone baking mat with a honeycomb pattern
6 × 2-in. (5-cm) dessert rings, 1½ in. (4 cm) deep
Vegetable mill
Electric hand beater
Immersion blender
6 × 2-in (5-cm) spiral silicone molds, 1½ in. (4 cm) deep
Thermometer
Kitchen torch

Ingredients

Tuiles
¼ cup (1¼ oz./35 g) confectioners' sugar
2½ tbsp (1¼ oz./35 g) unsalted butter
1 lightly beaten egg white
⅓ cup (1¼ oz./35 g) all-purpose flour
1 pinch of powdered yellow food coloring (optional)

Parsnip crème brûlée
3½ oz. (100 g) parsnips
1⅔ cups (400 ml) cream, minimum 35% fat
8 egg yolks
1½ tbsp (¾ oz./20 g) granulated sugar
1 pinch sea salt
Piment d'Espelette

Praline custard
6 egg yolks
Scant ½ cup (2¾ oz./80 g) granulated sugar
2 cups (500 ml) reduced fat milk
2 tbsp (30 g) praline paste

To serve
Brown sugar for sprinkling
1 Granny Smith apple
15-18 caramelized hazelnuts
A little crème pâtissière (optional)
Edible gold leaf

PREPARING THE TUILES
Preheat the oven to 325°F (160°C/Gas mark 3). Line a baking sheet with a silicone baking mat with a honeycomb pattern. Mix all the ingredients together until smooth. Spread the batter over the baking mat and bake in the oven for 6 minutes. Unmold and cut into 6 strips, ¾–1¼ in. (2–3 cm) wide and 6¼ in. (16 cm) long. Bake in the oven for an additional 3 minutes, then roll the strips around the 2-in. (5-cm) dessert rings. Let cool and harden. Leave the oven switched on but lower the temperature to 175°F (80°C/Gas mark ¼).

PREPARING THE PARSNIP CRÈME BRÛLÉE
Wash and peel the parsnips, cut them into chunks, and boil *à l'anglaise* (see technique p. 90). Drain, then pass through a vegetable mill. In a large heavy saucepan over medium heat, bring the cream to a boil. In the meantime, whisk the egg yolks with the sugar until pale. Drizzle the cream over the yolks and sugar mixture, whisking constantly. Add the pureed parsnips, process with an immersion blender, and season with the salt and a little piment d'Espelette. Pour some of the crème brûlée mixture into the spiral molds and bake for 20 minutes. Remove from the oven, let cool, then place in the freezer for 1 hour, so they are easier to unmold. Line a baking sheet with parchment paper and place the dessert rings on it. Divide the remaining crème brûlée mixture among them, pouring it to a depth of 1¼ in. (3 cm). Press heatproof plastic wrap over the surface and bake in the oven at 175°F (80°C/Gas mark ¼) for 45 minutes, until set. Let cool, then unmold the frozen spiral crème brûlées on top.

PREPARING THE PRALINE CUSTARD
In a mixing bowl, whisk the egg yolks with the sugar until pale. In a saucepan over medium heat, bring the milk to a boil with the praline paste, stirring to combine. Stir or whisk some of the hot milk mixture into the whisked yolks and sugar and return to the saucepan. Reduce the heat to low and stir constantly until the temperature reaches 185°F (85°C) and coats the back of a spoon. Strain the custard into a bowl, press plastic wrap over the surface to prevent a skin forming, let cool, and then chill in the refrigerator.

TO SERVE
Sprinkle a little brown sugar over the spiral tops of the crème brûlées and caramelize lightly with a kitchen torch. Place a crème brûlée in each serving dish or shallow bowl and surround with a tuile ring. Peel, core, and cut the apple into matchsticks and halve the hazelnuts. Spoon the praline custard around the crème brûlées, outlining a decorative shape with the crème pâtissière if wished, and add the halved hazelnuts. Top with a few apple matchsticks and a little edible gold leaf.

RUTABAGA SAUERKRAUT

Choucroute de rutabaga

Serves 6

Active time
20 minutes

Cooking time
40 minutes

Equipment
Rotating mandoline
slicer

Ingredients

8 rutabagas (swedes)

3 sweet onions

5 tbsp (2 oz./60 g)
goose or duck fat,
divided

1¼ cups (300 ml) dry
white Alsatian wine,
or other dry white wine

1¼ cups (300 ml) white
chicken stock

10 juniper berries

1 clove

2 fresh thyme sprigs,
plus extra for garnish

1 bay leaf

1 garlic clove, unpeeled

1 pinch sugar

Salt and freshly ground
pepper

PREPARING THE SAUERKRAUT

Wash and peel the rutabagas and peel the onions. Finely slice the onions (see technique p. 55).

Using the rotating mandoline slicer, cut the rutabaga into slices about ¾ in. (2 cm) wide and 6 in. (15 cm) long.

In a sauté pan or skillet, melt half the goose or duck fat and sweat the onions without letting them color. When they are very soft, deglaze the pan with the white wine. Let the wine reduce before pouring in the chicken stock. Let simmer for about 10 minutes and then set aside.

In a separate sauté pan or skillet, melt the remaining goose or duck fat and add the rutabaga strips with the juniper berries, clove, thyme, bay leaf, whole garlic clove, and sugar. Season with salt and pepper, cover with a lid, and cook for 10 minutes.

Stir the onions into the rutabagas and simmer for 10 minutes.

TO SERVE

Using two forks, pile the rutabaga sauerkraut into serving bowls and spoon over the cooking juices. Garnish with thyme sprigs.

BEET SALAD WITH TRUFFLE VINAIGRETTE

Salade de betteraves crues et cuites, vinaigrette truffée

Serves 10

Active time
2 hours

Cooking time
2 hours

Equipment
1¼-in. (3-cm) round cookie cutter
2 silicone baking mats
Fine-mesh sieve
Immersion blender
5½-in. (14-cm) tart ring

Ingredients

Raw and cooked beets
2 yellow beets
1 garlic clove, unpeeled
1 thyme sprig
3 tbsp (50 ml) olive oil
1 mini Chioggia beet
10 mini beets with their greens
2½ tbsp (1 oz./30 g) sugar
2 tbsp (25 g) butter
Fleur de sel
Freshly ground pepper

Bread chips
4 slices from a sandwich loaf, ¼ in. (5 mm) thick
4 tsp (20 g) melted butter

Garnishes
40 baby green Swiss chard leaves
40 baby beet leaves
4 organic eggs
10 quail eggs
1 bunch chives
15 baby potatoes

Truffle vinaigrette
½ tsp fine salt
¼ tsp freshly ground pepper
4 tsp (20 ml) sherry vinegar
2 tsp (10 ml) red wine vinegar
1 tbsp plus 2 tsp (25 ml) truffle *jus*
⅔ cup (150 ml) peanut oil
3 tbsp black truffle breakings

To serve
A few truffle shavings (optional)

PREPARING THE RAW AND COOKED BEETS

Preheat the oven to 350°F (180°C/Gas mark 4). Wrap the whole yellow beets, garlic clove, and thyme in a parchment paper package, drizzle over the olive oil, seal tightly, and bake for 1 hour. Unwrap the package, peel the cooked beets, and cut them into ¾-in. (2-cm) cubes. Finely slice the raw Chioggia beet and trim with the cookie cutter. Place the disks in a bowl of ice water. Place the mini beets in a sauté pan with the sugar, butter, salt, and pepper and half-fill the pan with water. Cover and cook over low heat until reduced and the beets are glazed but not colored. Reduce the oven temperature to 325°F (170°C/Gas mark 3).

PREPARING THE BREAD CHIPS

Using the cookie cutter, cut the bread slices into 10 disks and brush with the butter. Place them between two silicone mats and bake for a few minutes until pale golden. Set aside.

PREPARING THE GARNISHES

Wash and dry the Swiss chard and beet leaves. Hard-boil the hens' eggs in a saucepan of boiling water for 10 minutes. Peel and push them through a fine-mesh sieve. Fry the quail eggs in a non-stick skillet. Wash and finely chop or snip the chives (see Chefs' Notes p. 54). Turn the potatoes (see technique p. 78) and boil them *à l'anglaise* (see technique p. 90) until tender.

PREPARING THE TRUFFLE VINAIGRETTE

Place all the ingredients apart from the truffle breakings in a mixing bowl and combine using an immersion blender. Just before serving, stir in the truffle breakings and toss the raw and cooked beets with the vinaigrette, reserving a little to drizzle around the plates when serving.

TO SERVE

Place the tart ring on a serving plate and spoon in some of the sieved egg and chives in an even layer. Remove the ring and repeat with the other serving plates. Divide the beet salad seasoned with the vinaigrette among the servings and arrange the fried quail eggs, turned potatoes, bread chips, and truffle shavings, if using, attractively on top. Season with fleur de sel and freshly ground pepper and drizzle the reserved vinaigrette around the plates.

CARDAMOM-SCENTED BEETS WITH QUICK-SMOKED PIKE PERCH

Betterave à la cardamome et sandre fumé minute

Serves 10

Active time
2 hours

Marinating and drying time
36 hours

Cooking time
1 hour

Equipment
Mandoline
Round cookie cutter (size depends on size of the beets)
10 smoking cloches

Ingredients

Pike perch gravlax
1½ cups (14 oz./400 g) fine sea salt
1½ cups (14 oz./400 g) kosher salt
2 cups (14 oz./400 g) granulated sugar
2¼ lb. (1 kg) pike perch fillet
10 cardamom pods
1¼ cups (300 ml) beet juice

Beet disks
2 raw red round beets
Scant ½ cup (100 ml) aged wine vinegar
Scant ½ cup (100 ml) sherry vinegar
A few cardamom pods
Olive oil

Baby beets
1 bunch multicolored baby beets
2 garlic cloves
2 sprigs thyme
A little olive oil

To serve
Crème fraîche
1 handful red arroche (French spinach)
1 handful edible red oxalis (wood sorrel)
Hay

PREPARING THE PIKE PERCH GRAVLAX
This is done in two stages. In a large dish, mix the two types of salt with the sugar and press this over the fish until coated. Cover the dish with plastic wrap and refrigerate overnight. The next day, rinse the fish thoroughly to remove the salt and sugar and let dry on sheets of paper towel for 12 hours in the refrigerator. Lightly crush the cardamom pods and stir them into the beet juice. Return the pike perch to the dish, pour over the beet juice, and let marinate in the refrigerator overnight.

PREPARING THE BEET DISKS
Peel the beets and finely slice them on the mandoline. Trim the slices neatly with the cookie cutter. Combine the two vinegars in a mixing bowl, add the beet slices, and marinate for 12 hours in the refrigerator, at the same time as the pike perch is marinating for the second time. Drain the beet slices over a bowl to catch the marinade and set aside the slices. Lightly crush the cardamom pods. Transfer the marinade to a small heavy saucepan, add the cardamom pods, and reduce a little over low heat. Strain and whisk in sufficient olive oil to make a vinaigrette.

PREPARING THE BABY BEETS
Preheat the oven to 350°F (180°C/Gas mark 4). Cut some shavings from the baby beets using the mandoline and reserve in a bowl of ice water. Peel the garlic cloves and leave whole. Wrap up the remaining beets, garlic cloves, thyme, and a little olive oil in parchment paper packages and bake for about 45 minutes, until tender.

TO SERVE
Roll the beet disks into cones and fill with a little of the crème fraiche. Divide among serving plates. Finely slice the pike perch and arrange the slices attractively on the plates with the roasted baby beets. Garnish with a few red arroche and oxalis leaves and the reserved raw baby beet shavings. Just before serving, burn the hay and trap the smoke above the plate by placing a cloche over each one.

JERUSALEM ARTICHOKE RISOTTO IN A SHELL

Risotto de topinambour en coque de pain

Serves 6

Active time
1 hour

Cooking time
1 hour

Equipment
Rolling pin or metal tube
Immersion blender
Electric hand beater
Mandoline
Pot with deep-frying basket or deep fryer
Thermometer

Ingredients

Bread shells
½ cup (4½ oz./125 g) butter
6 slices from a sandwich loaf, about 1/16 in. (2 mm) thick

Jerusalem artichoke risotto
6 Jerusalem artichokes
1 shallot
7 tbsp (3½ oz./100 g) butter, divided
1 ⅔ cups (400 ml) hot white chicken stock
3 oz. (80 g) freshly grated Parmesan
¼ bunch chives
Salt and freshly ground pepper

Jerusalem artichoke puree
7 oz. (200 g) cooked Jerusalem artichokes
3 tbsp (2 oz./50 g) butter
Scant ¼ cup (50 ml) cream, minimum 35% fat
Salt and freshly ground pepper

Jerusalem artichoke chips
1 Jerusalem artichoke
Oil for frying

To serve
6 slices pancetta
6 scented geranium flowers and leaves
Balsamic vinegar (optional)

PREPARING THE BREAD SHELLS

Clarify the butter by melting it gently over low heat in a heavy saucepan. Skim off the froth, then pour the clear yellow layer of clarified butter into a jug, leaving behind the milky residue. You need 3½ oz. (100 g) clarified butter for the shells. Preheat the oven to 325°F (160°C/Gas mark 3). Cut the bread slices into 6 rectangles measuring 4 × 6 in. (10 × 15 cm). Cover a rolling pin with aluminum foil (or use a metal tube of similar diameter). Brush the bread with the clarified butter, shape the rectangles over the rolling pin, and bake for 20 minutes, until the bread is crisp and golden. Carefully remove the bread shells from the rolling pin.

PREPARING THE JERUSALEM ARTICHOKE RISOTTO

Wash, peel, and finely dice the artichokes into brunoise (see technique p. 60). Peel and finely chop the shallot (see technique p. 56). In a sauté pan or skillet over low heat, melt 4 tablespoons (2 oz./60 g) of the butter and sweat the shallot until softened and translucent. Add the diced artichokes, increase the heat to medium, and gradually add the chicken stock, a ladleful at a time, waiting until the stock has evaporated before adding more. Repeat until the artichokes are tender. Take the pan off the heat and stir in the Parmesan. Wash and chop or snip the chives (see Chefs' Notes p. 54), add with the remaining 3 tablespoons (1½ oz./40 g) butter, and season with salt and pepper. Fill the bread shells with the risotto and keep warm in a 200°F (100°C/Gas mark ¼) oven.

PREPARING THE JERUSALEM ARTICHOKE PUREE

Mash the artichokes and, using an immersion blender, process them with the butter until smooth. Season with salt and pepper. Whip the cream until it holds soft peaks and lightly fold in.

PREPARING THE JERUSALEM ARTICHOKE CHIPS

Peel and wash the artichoke and slice it finely on the mandoline. Pat the slices dry with paper towel. Heat an oil bath to 265°F (130°C) and deep-fry until golden. Drain on a plate lined with paper towel.

TO SERVE

Remove the shells from the oven and increase to 325°F (160°C/Gas mark 3). Line a baking sheet with parchment paper and place the pancetta slices on top. Cover with another sheet of parchment paper and place another baking sheet on top. Cook in the oven for 8 minutes. Shape a little of the artichoke puree into a rectangle in the center of each serving plate and add another swirl of puree to one side. Top with a risotto-filled bread shell, the geranium flowers and leaves, the artichoke chips, and the pancetta slices. Garnish the plates with drops of balsamic vinegar.

SALSIFY AND CRISP SWEETBREADS

Salsifis et ris de veau croustillant aux amandes

Serves 10

Active time
2 hours

Soaking time
1 hour

Cooking time
2 hours

Equipment
Skimmer
Immersion blender

Ingredients
10 × 6-oz. (180-g) lobes veal sweetbreads
2/3 cup (150 ml) white vinegar

Buttered almonds
1¼ sticks (5 oz./150 g) butter
1 cup (5 oz./150 g) natural (unskinned) almonds

Salsify
3 lb. (1.5 kg) salsify
1²/3 cups (400 ml) chicken stock
2²/3 sticks (10 oz./300 g) unsalted butter
A little olive oil
2/3 cup (150 ml) cream, minimum 35% fat
Oil for frying
Salt and freshly ground pepper

Shallots
10 French gray shallots
2 tsp (10 g) sugar
2 tsp (10 g) butter
1 pinch of fine salt

Breading
Flour for dredging
4 eggs
7 oz. (400 g) bread crumbs
1 cup (3½ oz./100 g) ground almonds
3½ oz. (100 g) freshly grated Parmesan
3 tbsp (2 oz./50 g) butter

To serve
1¼ cups (300 ml) veal *jus* flavored with dried fennel

PREPARING THE SWEETBREADS
Soak the sweetbread lobes for 1 hour in a large bowl of cold water with the vinegar added. Drain, place the sweetbreads in a large saucepan, and pour in enough cold water to cover. Bring to a boil, skim, and let simmer for 2 minutes. Drain and, while still hot, peel away the membranes and remove the fat and cartilage, taking care to leave the flesh intact. Pat dry with paper towel. Place on a plate with a weight on top and set aside in the refrigerator.

PREPARING THE BUTTERED ALMONDS
In a heavy saucepan, heat the butter, add the almonds, and cook until the butter is hazelnut brown. Lift out the almonds with a skimmer and drain on paper towel. Reserve the butter for preparing the *jus*.

PREPARING THE SALSIFY
Run cold water over the salsify, scrubbing off any dirt with a brush. Peel, set one salsify root aside, and cut the others into angled logs (see technique p. 64), 3 in. (8 cm) long. Reserve the trimmings. Bring the stock to a boil in a saucepan. In a sauté pan, melt the butter with a little olive oil and, when the butter is foaming, add the salsify logs and cook gently for 5 minutes. Stir in the stock and cook for an additional 20 minutes, until tender when pierced with the tip of a knife. Season with salt and pepper and set aside. Cook the trimmings with the cream in a saucepan over medium-low heat until reduced. Using an immersion blender, process until very smooth and light. Cut the reserved salsify into thin strips. Fry them in oil until lightly golden and crisp. Reserve a few for serving and crush the rest into coarse crumbs.

PREPARING THE SHALLOTS
Place the shallots in a sauté pan, pour in enough water to half-cover them, and add the sugar, butter, and salt. Bring to a simmer, reduce the heat, and cook until the shallots are caramelized. Drizzle over a little water.

PREPARING THE BREADED SWEETBREADS
Place the flour in a mixing bowl, beat the eggs in a separate bowl, and combine the bread crumbs, ground almonds, and Parmesan in a third bowl. Dust the sweetbreads with the flour, dip in the egg, and then coat in the dry ingredients (see technique p. 100). Melt the butter in a large skillet and fry the sweetbreads until golden and crisp all over.

TO SERVE
Pour the veal *jus* into a small saucepan and, over medium heat, gradually whisk in the browned butter reserved from cooking the almonds. Just before serving, dip the salsify logs in the salsify cream to half-coat them, press the salsify crumbs over the cream, and top with the reserved strips. Arrange the sweetbreads and salsify logs on serving plates with the glazed shallots and almonds. Drizzle the veal and butter *jus* around.

ROASTED CHERVIL ROOT WITH TRUFFLED *JUS*

Cerfeuils tubéreux rôtis au jus truffé

Serves 6

Active time
30 minutes

Cooking time
30 minutes

Equipment
Scouring pad
Silicone baking mat with a leaf pattern

Ingredients

Chervil root
2¼ lb. (1 kg) chervil root
Juice of 1 lemon
1¼ sticks (5 oz./150 g) butter, divided
¾ cup (200 ml) brown chicken stock
3½ oz. (100 g) chopped truffle
Salt and freshly ground pepper

Lacy leaves
Scant ½ cup (1¾ oz./50 g) all-purpose flour
3 tbsp plus 1 tsp (1¾ oz./50 g) melted butter
Scant ¼ cup (1¾ oz./50 g) egg white (about 1¾ whites)
½ tsp (2.5 g) smoked paprika

To serve
1 stalk of yellow celery
Leaves from 1 bunch chervil
4 tsp (20 ml) whipped cream

PREPARING THE CHERVIL ROOTS
Peel the chervil roots and, using a scouring pad, rub them into even shapes. Drizzle lightly with the lemon juice. In a large skillet, melt 1 stick plus 2 tablespoons (4½ oz./140 g) of the butter over medium heat and cook until it is hazelnut brown. Add the chervil roots and fry for about 10 minutes, or until golden brown all over. Season with salt and pepper and drain on a plate lined with paper towel. Add the chicken stock to the skillet used to fry the chervil roots, reduce the heat to low, and add the truffle and the remaining 2 teaspoons (10 g) of butter. Return the chervil roots to the pan and cook until the roots are glazed.

PREPARING THE LACY LEAVES
Preheat the oven to 325°F (160°C/Gas mark 3). Place the silicone mat on a baking sheet. In a medium bowl, whisk all the ingredients together. Using a spatula, spread the mixture evenly over the baking mat and bake for 6 minutes. Remove the leaves carefully from the mat once they are firm and cool enough to handle.

TO SERVE
Arrange the chervil roots in staggered rows in each serving dish. Finely chop the celery and wash the chervil leaves. Scatter the celery and chervil leaves over the roots and top with tiny dots of whipped cream. Decorate each serving with a lacy leaf.

CHINESE ARTICHOKE FRICASSEE WITH SPAETZLE AND CHESTNUTS

Fricassée de crosnes, spätzle et châtaignes

Serves 6

Active time
30 minutes

Cooking time
1 hour 10 minutes

Equipment
Fine-mesh sieve
Skimmer
Electric hand beater
Spaetzle grater with a slider basket

Ingredients

Chicken *jus*
1 lb. (500 g) chicken wings
7 oz. (200 g) shallots
2 onions
Olive oil
¼ cup (60 ml) soy sauce
2 thyme sprigs
Leaves from 1 bunch tarragon

Spaetzle
1²⁄₃ cups (7 oz./200 g) all-purpose flour
3 eggs
2 tbsp plus 2 tsp (40 ml) reduced fat milk
3 tbsp plus 2 tsp (2 oz./50 g) fromage blanc or ricotta
1 tsp (5 g) salt
½ tsp freshly grated nutmeg
4 tbsp (2 oz./60 g) butter, for reheating

Chinese artichoke fricassee
14 oz. (400 g) Chinese artichokes
2 cups (500 ml) white chicken stock
2 garlic cloves

Chestnuts
7 oz. (200 g) chestnuts

To serve
5 tbsp (3 oz./80 g) butter, divided
1 tbsp chopped parsley

PREPARING THE CHICKEN *JUS*
Preheat the oven to 350°F (180°C/Gas mark 4), spread the chicken wings in a roasting pan, and roast in the oven for about 20 minutes, or until golden. Peel and chop the shallots and onions (see technique p. 56). Heat a little olive oil in a large pot over medium heat and sweat the shallots and onions until softened. Add the chicken wings, stir well, and strain through a fine-mesh sieve to remove the fat. Return the chicken, shallots, and onions to the saucepan and deglaze with the soy sauce. Add the thyme, pour in enough cold water to cover the chicken, bring to a simmer, and cook for about 20 minutes, skimming the surface from time to time. Strain through a fine-mesh sieve and return the cooking liquid to the saucepan. Add the tarragon to infuse the *jus* and reduce over low heat so it thickens a little.

PREPARING THE SPAETZLE
In a mixing bowl, whisk the flour, eggs, milk, fromage blanc or ricotta, salt, and nutmeg together until smooth. Bring a large saucepan of water to a boil and prepare a bowl of ice water. Place the dough in the slider basket of a spaetzle grater and grate small pieces of the dough straight into the boiling water. Cook for 4–5 minutes, until the spaetzle float, remove them with a skimmer, and refresh briefly in the ice water to cool them. Set aside until ready to reheat in the butter.

PREPARING THE CHINESE ARTICHOKE FRICASSEE
Trim the tips of the Chinese artichokes and rinse under cold water. In a large saucepan, bring the chicken stock to a boil. Peel the garlic cloves and add them whole to the pan with the Chinese artichokes. Lower the heat under the pan and simmer for about 10 minutes until the artichokes are tender but still retain a little crunch. Drain the artichokes and garlic, crushing the cloves to a puree, and set aside until ready to reheat.

PREPARING THE CHESTNUTS
Using the tip of a small, sharp knife, cut an incision from one edge of the lighter side of each chestnut shell to the other, passing through the tip. Place the chestnuts in a large saucepan of cold water, bring to a boil, boil for 3 minutes, and then drain. Cool under cold water so you can crack and remove the outer shell and bitter membrane inside by pressing the chestnuts with your fingers.

TO SERVE
In a skillet over medium heat, melt the butter for reheating the spaetzle and sauté them for a few minutes, until golden and slightly puffed. In another skillet, melt half the butter until sizzling, add the chestnuts, and sauté them until golden. Brown the Chinese artichokes in the remaining butter in a third skillet with the crushed garlic and the parsley. Arrange the spaetzle, chestnuts, and Chinese artichokes attractively in a serving pan or dish and drizzle over the chicken *jus*.

GOURDS

ROASTED PUMPKIN WITH PEARS, FETA, AND PICKLED EGG

Potiron rôti, poire, feta et pickles d'œuf

Serves 6

Active time
50 minutes

Cooking time
35 minutes

Marinating time
24 hours

Equipment
100 ml pipette or small squeeze bottle
Mandoline

Ingredients

Pickled eggs
1 cup (250 ml) rice vinegar
2/3 cup (150 ml) soy sauce
1/2 cup (3½ oz./100 g) sugar
6 egg yolks

Mango sauce
1¼ tsp (4 g) cornstarch
5 oz. (150 g) mango coulis
1 tbsp (15 ml) cider vinegar
2½ tsp (10 g) sugar
Salt and freshly ground pepper

Pumpkin
3½–4½ lb. (1.5–2 kg) pumpkin
Olive oil for brushing
Maple syrup for brushing
Salt and freshly ground pepper

To serve
¾ oz. (20 g) pumpkin seeds
7 oz. (200 g) feta
1 pear
A few mizuna leaves (Japanese mustard greens)

PREPARING THE PICKLED EGGS
In a bowl, combine the rice vinegar, soy sauce, and sugar to make the marinade. Place the egg yolks in a container with a lid. Pour the marinade over them, ensuring they are covered, and let marinate in the refrigerator for 24 hours.

PREPARING THE MANGO SAUCE
Stir the cornstarch into a little cold water until smooth. In a saucepan over medium-high heat, heat the mango coulis with the vinegar, sugar, and diluted cornstarch. Bring to a boil, stirring constantly until thickened. Season with salt and pepper, let cool, and refrigerate in a pipette or squeeze bottle.

ROASTING THE PUMPKIN
Preheat the oven to 350°F (180°C/Gas mark 4). Cut the pumpkin into 6 slices. Brush the slices with olive oil, season with salt and pepper, and roast until tender, about 20 minutes. Just before the pumpkin is tender, brush the slices with a little maple syrup to glaze them.

TO ASSEMBLE AND SERVE
Reduce the oven temperature to 300°F (150°C/Gas mark 2). Line a baking sheet with parchment paper, spread the pumpkin seeds over it, and toast for 15 minutes. In the meantime, crumble the feta into a bowl. Peel and core the pear and, using the mandoline, slice it finely. Drain the eggs from the marinade and arrange with all the other components attractively on serving plates. Pipe the mango sauce into small mounds on the plates and garnish with a few mizuna leaves.

SWEET AND SAVORY SQUASH AND VEGETABLE CASSEROLE

Cocotte de potimarron et légumes étuvés, jus de raisin en aigre-doux

Serves 6

Active time
2 hours

Marinating time
1 hour

Cooking time
2 hours

Equipment
Mandoline
Grill pan
Immersion blender

Ingredients

Marinated quince
1 quince
¾ cup (200 ml) water
2 tbsp (1 oz./25 g) sugar
3 tbsp (50 ml) white vinegar

Vegetables and fruit
12 young fresh carrots
3½ oz. (100 g) green grapes
9 baby artichokes
1 large kuri or orange Hubbard squash
9 cooking pears, preferably Martin Sec
1 stick plus 2 tbsp (5¼ oz./150 g) butter
Juice of 1 lemon, plus extra for the artichoke water
18 fresh chestnuts (or use frozen or canned whole chestnuts)

Potatoes
9 oz. (250 g) baby potatoes
4–6 garlic cloves
7 tbsp (3½ oz./100 g) butter
A few thyme sprigs

Sweet and savory sauce (gastrique)
¼ cup (2 oz./50 g) sugar
3 tbsp (50 ml) sherry vinegar
1 cup (250 ml) grape juice
3 tbsp (50 g) lightly salted butter, diced

To garnish
Leaves of 1 head late Treviso red chicory
2 oz. (50 g) red vein cress

PREPARING THE MARINATED QUINCE

Wash, peel, and finely slice the quince using the mandoline and place in a bowl. In a medium saucepan, bring the water to a boil with the sugar and vinegar to make a light syrup. Pour over the quince and let marinate for 1 hour.

PREPARING THE VEGETABLES AND FRUIT

Wash and peel the carrots and grapes. Turn the artichokes (see technique p. 70) and reserve them in a bowl of water with a little lemon juice added. Wash but do not peel the squash and pears. Quarter the squash, remove the seeds, and cut the flesh into cubes. Cut the carrots, pears, and artichokes in half lengthwise and core the pears. In a covered sauté pan over low heat, cook the carrots, artichokes, and pears separately (in that order) until tender, adding one-third of the butter and lemon juice to the pan each time. When cooking the artichokes and pears, reduce the cooking liquid so it glazes and lightly browns them. If using fresh chestnuts, preheat the oven to 350°F (180°C/Gas mark 4). Using a sharp knife, cut a long slit in the shell on the rounded side of each one. Place the chestnuts on a baking sheet and roast in the oven for about 15 minutes, until the slits in the shells open. Carefully snap off the shells and remove the skin while still hot. Cut each chestnut in half and brown on the grill pan.

PREPARING THE POTATOES

Wash the potatoes and parboil them whole for 15 minutes. Peel and crush the garlic cloves and cut the potatoes in half. In a skillet over medium-high heat, melt the butter and, when it is foaming, sauté the potatoes with the garlic and thyme sprigs.

PREPARING THE SWEET AND SAVORY SAUCE

In a large saucepan, dissolve the sugar in the vinegar. Pour in the grape juice and bring to a boil. Using an immersion blender, incorporate the butter, processing until the sauce has a syrupy texture and is thick enough to coat the vegetables.

TO SERVE

Arrange the different fruits and vegetables attractively in individual serving dishes. Roll the marinated quince slices and place on top. Garnish with a few leaves of late Treviso red chicory and red vein cress. Drizzle the sauce over each serving.

CHEFS' NOTES

Small, firm Martin Sec pears are an heirloom variety. If unavailable, try Seckel, Bartlett, or Forelle pears.

ROASTED BUTTERNUT AND LANGOUSTINE BISQUE

Butternut confit et bisque de langoustine

Serves 6

Active time
1½ hours

Cooking time
55 minutes

Equipment
Pestle
Fine-mesh sieve
Grill pan
3-in. (8-cm) round cookie cutter

Ingredients

Langoustines
6 raw langoustines or jumbo shrimp

Langoustine bisque
7 oz. (200 g) tomatoes
3½ oz. (100 g) onions
3½ oz. (100 g) shallots
2 garlic cloves
⅓ cup (80 ml) olive oil
1 lb. (500 g) langoustine or jumbo shrimp shells, tails, and heads
1 cup (250 ml) Sauvignon blanc, or other dry white wine
3 tbsp (50 ml) Cognac
4 tsp (20 ml) Noilly Prat
1 bunch tarragon, leaves chopped
2 sprigs thyme, leaves chopped
1 bouquet garni
2 cups (500 ml) cream, minimum 35% fat
1 tbsp tomato paste

Roasted butternut
3 lb. (1.5 kg) butternut
Olive oil
Salt and freshly ground pepper

Butternut risotto
½ onion
7 tbsp (4 oz./110 g) butter, diced and well chilled, divided
2½ cups (600 ml) hot fish stock
2 oz. (60 g) freshly grated Parmesan
½ bunch chives
Salt and freshly ground pepper

To serve
Olive oil for frying
Mixed herb sprigs such as borage, chervil, and tarragon

PREPARING THE LANGOUSTINES

Remove the heads from the langoustines and peel away the shells, leaving the tails attached. Refrigerate the heads and tails until ready to serve, reserving the carcasses to add to those for the bisque.

PREPARING THE LANGOUSTINE BISQUE

Wash the tomatoes, peel the onions and shallots, and cut all three into brunoise (see technique p. 60). Peel and crush the garlic cloves. Pour the olive oil into a pot over high heat. Sear the shellfish carcasses, then add the onions and shallots. Deglaze with the white wine and reduce before adding the Cognac and carefully flambéing. When the flames have subsided, pour in the Noilly Prat. Using a pestle, crush the carcasses to extract as much flavor as possible. Add the tomatoes, herbs, and bouquet garni, and stir in the cream and tomato paste. Reduce the heat and simmer for 20 minutes. Strain the bisque through a fine-mesh sieve and keep warm over a hot water bath.

PREPARING THE ROASTED BUTTERNUT

Preheat the oven to 275°F (140°C/Gas mark 1). Peel the butternut and cut 6 × ¾-in. (2-cm) slices, reserving the rest and the trimmings for the risotto. Brush the slices with oil and sear them in a grill pan to mark them with a crisscross pattern. Season and transfer to the oven and cook for about 20 minutes, until the slices are tender. Keep warm.

PREPARING THE BUTTERNUT RISOTTO

Cut the remaining butternut and its trimmings into brunoise (see technique p. 60). Peel and chop the onion finely. Melt 3 tablespoons (50 g) of the butter in a large skillet over medium heat and sweat the onion with the diced butternut without letting it color. Gradually add the fish stock, letting each addition of stock evaporate completely before adding more, continuing until the butternut is tender. Stir in the Parmesan to thicken the risotto and then stir in the remaining butter. Wash and chop or snip the chives (see Chefs' Notes p. 54) and stir in. Season with salt and pepper.

TO SERVE

Drizzle a little olive oil into a skillet over high heat and briefly cook the langoustine tails and heads until they turn pink and their flesh is opaque. Lay a slice of roasted butternut in the center of each serving bowl and spoon a little risotto on top. Add a langoustine tail, with the head alongside, and garnish with small herb sprigs. Serve the bisque in a jug, pouring it around the butternut at the last moment.

GRILLED PATTYPAN SQUASH WITH FENNEL CAVIAR AND FOCACCIA

Pâtissons grillés et focaccia au fenouil

Serves 4

Active time
1 hour

Rising time
12 hours + 1 hour

Cooking time
1 hour

Equipment
Sous vide bag and food vacuum sealer machine
Steam oven or steamer
Immersion blender
Mandoline
Grill pan

Ingredients

Fennel focaccia
½ oz. (12 g) fresh yeast
1⅓ cups (310 ml) lukewarm water
3¼ cups (14 oz./400 g) all-purpose flour
2½ oz. (75 g) potato flakes
2 tsp (10 g) fine sea salt
3 tbsp (50 ml) olive oil
Dried wild fennel seeds for sprinkling
Fleur de sel

Fennel caviar
1 fennel bulb
¾ cup (200 ml) olive oil
1 tsp fennel seeds
2 garlic cloves
2 thyme sprigs
Fine sea salt

Raw pattypan squash
4 yellow pattypan squash
4 green pattypan squash

Raw fennel
2 mini fennel bulbs

Grilled pattypan squash
4 yellow pattypan squash
8 green pattypan squash
Peanut oil for the grill pan
Fine sea salt

PREPARING THE FENNEL FOCACCIA

Crumble the yeast into the lukewarm water and let dissolve. In a mixing bowl, combine the flour, potato flakes, and salt, and pour in the yeast and water. Using your hands, knead to make a smooth dough. Cover and let rise in the refrigerator for 12 hours. Line a baking sheet with parchment paper. Punch down the dough, press it out evenly over the baking sheet, cover, and let rise at room temperature for 1 hour. Preheat the oven to 400°F (200°C/Gas mark 6). Press your fingers into the dough to make dimples, brush generously with olive oil, and sprinkle with fennel seeds and fleur de sel. Bake for 25 minutes until golden brown.

PREPARING THE FENNEL CAVIAR

Wash and cut the fennel bulb into quarters. Place all the ingredients in a sous vide bag, seal, and cook in a steam oven at 203°F (95°C) or steamer for about 20 minutes, until very tender. Open the bag and drain the fennel, reserving the liquid. Place the fennel pieces in a mixing bowl and, using an immersion blender, process until smooth, adding some of the cooking liquid if needed. You may also need to strain the puree.

PREPARING THE RAW PATTYPAN SQUASH

Wash the pattypan squash and, using the mandoline, cut into thin slices. Reserve in a bowl of ice water.

PREPARING THE RAW FENNEL

Wash the fennel bulbs and, using the mandoline, cut into thin slices. Reserve in a bowl of ice water.

PREPARING THE GRILLED PATTYPAN SQUASH

Wash the squash. Cut the yellow pattypan squash lengthwise into about 3 slices each. Cut the green pattypan squash into quarters. Heat a grill pan, brush it with the oil, and grill the pieces of squash on both sides to scorch with a crisscross pattern. Season with salt to taste.

TO SERVE

Cut the focaccia into long thin slices and toast quickly on a grill pan or in a toaster or oven. Spread the slices generously with the fennel caviar and arrange the raw and grilled pattypan squash on top with the raw fennel.

SEEDED SPAGHETTI SQUASH COOKIES

Sablés de courge spaghetti aux graines

**Makes about
30 cookies**

Active time

20 minutes

Cooking time

30 minutes

Equipment

Steam oven or steamer

2-in. (5-cm) round cookie
cutter

Ingredients

Seeds

2 oz. (50 g) pumpkin
seeds

2 tbsp (20 g) flaxseeds

1 tbsp (10 g) sesame
seeds

1 tbsp (10 g) nigella
seeds

Cookie dough

1 lb. (450 g) spaghetti
squash

3 oz. (90 g) grated
Comté, or other fruity
hard cheese

3 oz. (90 g) freshly
grated Parmesan

1²/₃ cups (5 oz./150 g)
gram (chickpea) flour

1¼ cups (5 oz./150 g)
cornstarch

2 tsp (10 g) baking
powder

2 tbsp garam masala

Salt and freshly ground
white pepper

PREPARING THE SEEDS

Preheat the oven to 300°F (150°C/Gas mark 2). Line a baking sheet with
parchment paper. Combine all of the seeds, spread them over the baking
sheet, and toast for about 10 minutes. Remove from the sheet and let cool.

PREPARING THE COOKIE DOUGH

Cut the spaghetti squash in half lengthwise. Using a spoon, scoop out the
seeds and then scrape out the flesh with a fork. Steam the flesh for about
10 minutes until tender (see technique p. 92). Let cool, place in a mixing bowl,
and stir in the grated cheeses, chickpea flour, cornstarch, seeds, baking
powder, and garam masala. When evenly combined, season with salt and
pepper, and press together with your hands to make a dough.

BAKING THE COOKIES

Increase the oven temperature to 350°F (180°C/Gas mark 4). Re-line the
baking sheet with clean parchment paper. On a lightly floured work surface,
roll the dough to a thickness of about ¾ in. (2 cm) and cut out disks using the
cookie cutter. Place on the baking sheet and bake for about 10 minutes, until
lightly golden. Transfer to a rack and let cool. Serve as an accompaniment
to aperitifs or a soup.

KABOCHA SQUASH BAKED IN A RICE COOKER

Kabocha cuite entière dans un cuiseur à riz

Serves 6

Active time
10 minutes

Cooking time
30 minutes

Equipment
Rice cooker

Ingredients

1 Japanese kabocha squash

6 cups (1.5 liters) sparkling water or soda water (see Chefs' Notes)

3 tbsp (50 ml) extra-virgin olive oil

Fleur de sel

Timut pepper

1 tbsp soy sauce (optional), for serving

Thoroughly wash the kabocha squash and cut off the top to form a lid.

Pour the sparkling water into the rice cooker, place the squash inside with its top, and cook for about 30 minutes until tender. To check for doneness, insert the tip of a knife into the squash flesh.

As the squash cooks, the seeds will flavor its flesh. Once cooked, however, scoop out the seeds with a spoon. Season the flesh with the olive oil, salt, and pepper.

Serve whole, adding a tablespoon of soy sauce if wished.

CHEFS' NOTES

Sparkling water preserves humidity and allows the squash to retain its texture and flavor as it cooks. Non-carbonated mineral water can also be used, though.

CHAYOTE SALAD WITH SPICY CARIBBEAN SAUCE

Salade de chayottes, sauce chien

Serves 6

Active time
30 minutes

Cooking time
5 minutes

Equipment
Food safe disposable gloves

Ingredients

Chayote salad
5 chayotes
3 carrots
3 tbsp (50 ml) sesame oil
Fleur de sel

Spicy Caribbean sauce
4 sweet, mild chili peppers
1 hot habanero chili pepper
1 red onion
2 garlic cloves
2 oz. (50 g) fresh ginger
1 bunch flat-leaf parsley
1 bunch cilantro
1 bunch scallions
3 limes
Scant ½ cup (100 ml) grapeseed oil
3 tbsp (40 ml) sesame oil
¾ cup (200 ml) mineral water

PREPARING THE CHAYOTE SALAD
Wash and peel the chayotes and carrots, and cut them into thin julienne strips (see technique p. 58). Combine the two and season with the sesame oil and fleur de sel. Chill until serving.

PREPARING THE SPICY CARIBBEAN SAUCE
Wear food safe disposable gloves to protect your hands when preparing the chili peppers. Halve the chili peppers, remove the membranes and seeds inside, and cut into brunoise (see technique p. 60). Peel and chop the onion and garlic. Peel and grate the ginger. Set aside 1 sprig each of parsley and cilantro and chop the rest (see technique p. 54). Slice the scallions, grate the lime zest and squeeze the juice. Combine all the ingredients in a mixing bowl with the grapeseed and sesame oils. Bring the mineral water to a boil, then gradually whisk or stir it in.

TO SERVE
Dress the salad with the sauce and serve it in bowls or soup plates, garnished with the reserved parsley and cilantro leaves.

CHEFS' NOTES

The sauce can be made ahead and stored in a covered container in the refrigerator.

Choose the chili peppers according to their level of heat on the Scoville scale.

CRUCIFEROUS VEGETABLES

SAVOY CABBAGE PARCELS
WITH CONSOMMÉ AND BROWN SHRIMP

Chou vert frisé, consommé cristallin aux crevettes grises

Serves 6

Active time
30 minutes

Cooking time
1½ hours

Equipment
Muslin cloth
Pot with deep-frying
basket or deep fryer
Thermometer

Ingredients
Vinegar
2 Savoy cabbages
3½ oz. (100 g) fresh
ginger
2 carrots
1 bunch scallions
2 garlic cloves
7 oz. (200 g) firm tofu
10 oz. (300 g) whole
brown shrimp, or small
North Atlantic shrimp,
unpeeled and cooked
1 bunch Thai scallions
1 bunch cilantro
1 lemongrass stalk
Scant ½ cup (100 ml)
soy sauce
3 tbsp (50 ml) fish sauce
(such as Vietnamese phu
quoc)
1½ tbsp (20 g) tomato
paste
6 cups (1.5 liters) mineral
water
1 tbsp coriander seeds
1 tbsp peppercorns
2 tbsp (1 oz./30 g) butter
4 tsp (10 g) all-purpose
flour
4 cups (1 liter)
grapeseed oil, plus extra
for the cabbage

PREPARING THE VEGETABLES AND FILLING

Wash and peel all the vegetables in water with vinegar added, allowing 3 tablespoons (50 ml) vinegar for every 4 cups (1 liter) of water. Peel off the dark green outer leaves of the cabbage and set them aside for the consommé. Peel the ginger, reserving the peel for the consommé. Cut the carrots into brunoise (see technique p. 60) and chop the white part of the scallions (see technique p. 56), reserving the green tops. Finely grate the ginger and garlic cloves. Combine in a small bowl, cover with plastic wrap, and refrigerate. Select 6 whole cabbage leaves and boil them *à l'anglaise* (see technique p. 90) in a large saucepan; they should remain crisp. Let cool, drain on a dish cloth, then wrap in the cloth and place in the refrigerator. Finely slice the remaining cabbage. Drain the tofu and cut it into 1¼-in. (3-cm) cubes. Chill in the refrigerator on a plate lined with paper towel to absorb any remaining liquid. Set aside 18 of the cooked shrimp to be fried for the garnish. Peel the remaining shrimp, reserving the heads, tails, and shells for the consommé, rinse under cold water, and set aside until ready to serve. Slice the Thai scallion lengthwise into very thin strips about 4 in. (10 cm) long. Place in a bowl of cold water and chill in the refrigerator until they curl. Cut off the cilantro stems and set aside a few leaves for garnish. Cut the lemongrass stalk into angled slices (see technique p. 64).

PREPARING THE CONSOMMÉ

Heat a little oil in a large saucepan and color the green cabbage leaves. Add the shrimp heads, tails, and shells and the ginger trimmings. Deglaze with the soy sauce and fish sauce. Add the lemongrass, scallion green tops, cilantro stalks, and tomato paste. Pour in the mineral water and stir in the coriander seeds and peppercorns. Bring to a gentle simmer and cook for 45 minutes. Remove from the heat, let rest for 10 minutes, and then strain through a muslin cloth into a large bowl without pressing down on the ingredients. Reserve at room temperature.

PREPARING THE CABBAGE PARCELS

In a medium skillet over low-medium heat, melt the butter and sweat the carrots and the chopped white part of the scallions without letting them color. Stir in the garlic, ginger, and sliced cabbage and pour in a scant ½ cup (100 ml) of the consommé. Simmer gently over low heat until well softened, then set aside. Divide the softened vegetables among the 6 blanched cabbage leaves, each placed on a sheet of plastic wrap. Fold the cabbage leaves around the filling to make 2½ × 1½-in. (6 × 4-cm) parcels, tucking in the edges of the leaves and enclosing the parcels in the plastic wrap so they keep their shape.

PREPARING THE FRIED TOFU, THAI SCALLIONS, AND SHRIMP

Coat the tofu cubes in the flour. Drain the Thai scallion curls and pat dry. In a fryer, heat the grapeseed oil to 340°F (170°C). Fry the tofu first, followed by the Thai scallion curls, and finally the 18 reserved shrimp, taking care not to splatter yourself. Drain them on plates lined with sheets of paper towel.

TO SERVE

Remove the plastic wrap from the cabbage parcels and place one in each soup plate or large bowl. Top with the fried tofu, Thai scallions, and shrimp. Divide the remaining peeled, cooked shrimp between the 6 bowls, arranging them around the cabbage parcel. Pour the consommé around using a teapot. Just before serving, garnish with the cilantro leaves.

CHEFS' NOTES

Gently simmer the consommé, without letting it boil, to ensure it remains a lovely clear amber color.

CAULIFLOWER THREE WAYS

Déclinaison de chou-fleur, rôti grenobloise, mousse et taboulé multicolore

Serves 6

Active time
1½ hours

Chilling time
1 hour

Cooking time
40 minutes

Equipment
Food processor
Electric hand beater
6 × 2-in. (5-cm) tartlet rings
Immersion blender

Ingredients

Cauliflower mousse
14 oz. (400 g) cauliflower
3½ sheets (7 g) gold bloom gelatin
Generous ½ cup (140 ml) whipping cream, minimum 35% fat

Multicolored cauliflower tabbouleh
½ orange cauliflower
½ green cauliflower
½ purple cauliflower
1 bunch cilantro
Finely grated zest and juice of 1 lime
Scant ½ cup (100 ml) olive oil
Fine sea salt and freshly ground pepper

Caper sauce
1 lemon
1 stick (4 oz./120 g) butter
2 slices of bread from a sandwich loaf
2 tbsp (15 g) capers

Pan-roasted cauliflower
1 cauliflower
1 stick plus 2 tbsp (5¼ oz./150 g) lightly salted butter

Cauliflower and tahini puree
14 oz. (400 g) cauliflower
3½ tbsp (2 oz./50 g) butter
3 tbsp (45 ml) tahini
Salt and freshly ground pepper

To serve
3½ oz. (100 g) samphire
6 caper berries with stems

PREPARING THE CAULIFLOWER MOUSSE

Wash and chop the cauliflower and, in a saucepan, boil *à l'anglaise* (see technique p. 90). Soften the gelatin in a bowl of cold water. Drain the cauliflower and, while still hot, process to a smooth puree (you should have about 11½ oz./325 g puree). Squeeze the excess water from the gelatin and stir it into the hot cauliflower puree until melted. Let the puree cool to room temperature but not set. Using an electric hand beater, whisk the cream until it holds soft peaks and fold into the cauliflower puree using a flexible spatula. Set the tartlet rings on a baking sheet lined with parchment paper, pour in the cauliflower puree and chill for 1 hour until set.

PREPARING THE MULTICOLORED CAULIFLOWER TABBOULEH

Wash all three cauliflower halves and, using a box grater, grate them on the wide-holed side into a bowl. Wash and finely chop the cilantro and stir in with the lime zest and juice. Season with the olive oil, salt, and pepper.

PREPARING THE CAPER SAUCE

Peel the lemon, removing all the white pith, and cut out the segments leaving the membrane behind. Dice the lemon flesh. Clarify the butter by heating it gently in a heavy saucepan over low heat. Skim off the froth, then pour the clear yellow layer of clarified butter into a jug, leaving behind the milky residue. Cut the bread into ¼-in. (5-mm) dice and fry in the clarified butter until golden. Drain on a plate lined with paper towel. Combine the diced lemon and capers and reserve the bread croutons separately.

PREPARING THE PAN-ROASTED CAULIFLOWER

Wash and cut the cauliflower into 6 large florets, reserving a few florets for garnish. In a large skillet over medium-heat, melt the butter, add the cauliflower, and pan-roast the florets until just tender, basting regularly with the butter. This should take about 15 minutes, depending on the size of the florets. When the cauliflower is cooked, add the caper sauce. Keep warm.

PREPARING THE CAULIFLOWER AND TAHINI PUREE

Wash and chop the cauliflower. In a saucepan, boil *à l'anglaise* until tender. Drain and process to a puree with the butter and tahini. Season with salt and pepper and adjust the consistency by adding a little water if necessary.

TO SERVE

Bring a saucepan of unsalted water to a boil and add the samphire. As soon as the water returns to a boil, drain and immerse the samphire in a bowl of ice water to prevent further cooking. Spoon a little of the cauliflower and tahini puree onto each serving plate and add the roasted cauliflower. Scatter over the reserved bread croutons. Unmold a cauliflower mousse onto each plate and cover with the tabbouleh. Garnish with the samphire, a few sliced raw cauliflower florets, and the caper berries.

ROASTED BROCCOLI WITH BOTTARGA AND CAESAR DRESSING

Brocoli rôti, poutargue et sauce césar

Serves 4

Active time
45 minutes

Cooking time
30 minutes

Equipment
Food processor

Ingredients

Broccoli
1 large head broccoli
7 tbsp (3½ oz./100 g) butter

Caesar dressing
2 eggs
¾ oz. (20 g) freshly grated Parmesan
½ oz. (15 g) anchovy fillets
3 tbsp (40 ml) lemon juice
2 tsp (10 ml) Worcestershire sauce
Leaves of ¼ bunch tarragon
Leaves of ¼ bunch basil
½ cup minus 1 tbsp (100 ml) olive oil
3 tbsp (40 ml) heavy cream, if needed

To serve
2 oz. (50 g) bottarga, finely grated

PREPARING THE BROCCOLI

Wash the head of broccoli and blanch it in a saucepan of boiling salted water for 30 seconds (see technique p. 88). Drain and cool by running cold water over it. Heat the butter in a small saucepan until it melts and turns golden brown. Be careful not to let it become too dark.

Preheat the oven to 350°F (180°C/Gas mark 4) and line a rimmed baking sheet with parchment paper. Place the broccoli on the baking sheet, pour over the browned butter, and roast for 20 minutes. Check the color and pierce the broccoli stem with the tip of a pointed knife to test for doneness.

PREPARING THE CAESAR DRESSING

Hard-boil one of the eggs, then halve, remove the yolk, and place it in the bowl of the food processor. Separate the other egg and add the yolk to the bowl. Process together the raw egg yolk, cooked yolk, Parmesan, and anchovy fillets until smooth. Add the lemon juice, Worcestershire sauce, and tarragon and basil leaves, and process again. Gradually whisk in the oil until incorporated and, if necessary, thin the dressing with the cream.

TO SERVE

Serve the roasted broccoli with the Caesar dressing and sprinkle with the grated bottarga.

MAPLE-GLAZED BRUSSELS SPROUTS WITH CRISPY ONION AND BACON

Choux de Bruxelles au sirop d'érable, crispy d'oignon et de lard fumé

Serves 6

Active time
30 minutes

Freezing time
20–30 minutes

Drying time
20 minutes

Cooking time
15 minutes

Equipment
Food slicer

Ingredients

Crispy onion and bacon
7 oz. (200 g) bacon, in one piece
2 white onions

Brussels sprouts
36 Brussels sprouts
2½ tsp (10 g) coarse sea salt
1 stick plus 2 tbsp (5 oz./150 g) lightly salted butter
1 cup (250 ml) maple syrup

To serve
A few flat-leaf parsley sprigs
3 tbsp (50 ml) olive oil
Fleur de sel
Freshly ground pepper

PREPARING THE CRISPY ONION AND BACON

Place the bacon and onions in the freezer for 20–30 minutes so they are easier to slice. Preheat the oven to 300°F (150°C/Gas mark 2) and line a baking sheet with parchment paper. Remove the bacon and onions from the freezer and peel the onions. Using the slicer, cut the bacon and onions into paper thin slices, about $\frac{1}{16}$ in. (1–2 mm) thick. Spread them on the baking sheet, cover with another sheet of parchment paper, and dry out in the oven until browned and crisp. This will take about 20 minutes, but check regularly.

PREPARING THE BRUSSELS SPROUTS

Wash the Brussels sprouts and carefully remove the outer leaves, reserving them for decoration. In a saucepan of boiling salted water, cook the sprouts *à l'anglaise* (see technique p. 90), ensuring that they retain their crunch. Drain, reserving the cooking liquid to blanch the leaves for decoration, if wished. Refresh the sprouts under cold water. Blanch the leaves reserved for decoration. Slice the sprouts in half lengthwise. In a large skillet, melt the butter and cook until it turns a golden brown. Add the halved sprouts, flat side down, and fry until browned. Deglaze with the maple syrup, spooning the pan juices regularly over the sprouts.

TO SERVE

Season the Brussels sprouts with salt and pepper and arrange them on serving plates. Scatter the browned bacon, onion, and parsley sprigs over them. Finally, if using, brush the reserved outer leaves of the sprouts with the olive oil to give them a glossy finish and use to decorate the dish.

ROMANESCO PATTIES AND PUREE WITH FLAME-SEARED MACKEREL

Galettes de chou romanesco, purée verte et maquereau à la flamme

Serves 6

Active time
40 minutes

Marinating time
1 hour

Cooking time
40 minutes

Equipment
Blender
Kitchen torch

Ingredients

Mackerel
3 mackerel
1¼ cups (300 ml) ponzu sauce

Romanesco puree
1 lb. (500 g) Romanesco
5 tbsp (2½ oz./70 g) unsalted butter
2½ oz. (70 g) freshly grated Parmesan
Fine sea salt and freshly ground pepper

Romanesco patties
1 lb. (500 g) Romanesco
2 scallions
1 garlic clove
¾ cup (200 ml) olive oil, divided
10 mint leaves
2 tbsp (20 g) all-purpose flour, plus more for coating
2 eggs, lightly beaten
1 tsp chopped oregano
Salt and freshly ground pepper

Pistachio-lemon sauce
1 lemongrass stalk
1¼ cups (300 ml) water
Generous 1 cup (5 oz./150 g) pistachios
Scant ½ cup (100 ml) fish stock
1 tbsp (15 g) grated fresh ginger
Scant ½ cup (100 ml) cream, minimum 35% fat
Scant ½ cup (100 ml) lemon juice
Finely grated zest of 1 lime
Salt and freshly ground pepper

To serve
18 cooked romanesco florets
2 tsp (5 g) matcha green tea powder

PREPARING THE MACKEREL

Fillet the mackerel, taking care to remove all pin bones. Place in a dish, pour over the ponzu sauce, cover with plastic wrap, and marinate for 1 hour in the refrigerator.

PREPARING THE ROMANESCO PUREE

Wash and chop the romanesco and cook in a saucepan of boiling salted water until tender. Drain and blend to a puree with the butter and Parmesan. Season with salt and pepper, let cool, and refrigerate until serving.

PREPARING THE ROMANESCO PATTIES

Wash and chop the romanesco and cook in a saucepan of boiling salted water until just tender. Drain, place in a mixing bowl, and crush roughly with a fork. Peel and chop the scallions (see technique p. 56). Peel and crush the garlic in a garlic press. Heat 3 tablespoons (50 ml) of the olive oil in a small skillet over medium heat and lightly sauté the scallions and garlic. Wash and finely chop the mint leaves. When the scallions and garlic have cooled, stir them into the crushed romanesco with the flour, eggs, oregano, and mint. Season with salt and pepper. Using your hands, roll into 12–18 balls, about 1½ in. (4 cm) in diameter, and flatten them slightly. Spread flour on a plate and coat the patties with it. Heat the remaining olive oil in a skillet or sauté pan and, working in batches if necessary, fry the patties until golden, turning them regularly. Drain on plates lined with paper towel and keep warm.

PREPARING THE PISTACHIO-LEMON SAUCE

Wash and finely slice the lemongrass. Place in a small saucepan, add the water, and bring to a boil for 3 minutes. Drain, reserving the lemongrass infused water. In a skillet over medium heat, roast the pistachios without letting them brown. Blend the pistachios to a paste with the lemongrass-infused water. In a saucepan over low heat, warm the fish stock, and stir in the ginger and cream. Pour the liquid into a blender and process with the pistachio paste. Return to the saucepan and cook over low heat for 10 minutes, stirring from time to time. Strain the sauce through a fine sieve, season with salt and pepper, and stir in the lemon juice and lime zest according to personal taste.

TO SERVE

Drain the mackerel from the marinade and lightly cook in a skillet, flesh side down. Finish cooking the skin using a kitchen torch, taking care not to overcook the fish. Place a little romanesco puree onto each serving plate and add a mackerel fillet, 2 or 3 romanesco patties, and a few florets. Spoon the pistachio sauce alongside and sprinkle a little matcha green tea powder around the edge of each plate.

RED CABBAGE PARCELS WITH BEER-BRAISED APPLES

Pomponnettes de chou rouge et pommes braisées à la bière

Serves 12

Active time
2 hours

Cooking time
1 hour 20 minutes

Equipment
Fine-mesh sieve
Melon baller

Ingredients

Red cabbage parcels
2 red cabbages
¾ cup (200 ml) white vinegar
6 Royal Gala apples, or other red-skinned crisp apples
Juice of 1 lemon
1½ sticks (6 oz./180 g) lightly salted butter
3 cups (750 ml) brown ale of your choice
1 thyme sprig
1 bay leaf
Fleur de sel
Freshly ground pepper

To serve
4 Royal Gala apples
3 tbsp (1¾ oz./50 g) butter, divided
A little brown ale

PREPARING THE RED CABBAGE PARCELS

Remove the outer cabbage leaves and set aside 12 large, undamaged leaves. Finely slice the remainder, reserving the trimmings. Bring a large pot of salted water to a boil with the vinegar and blanch the sliced cabbage. Drain but do not refresh. Peel and core the apples and cut them into large dice, reserving the peel and trimmings. Toss the diced apple with the lemon juice to prevent discoloration. Bring a large pot of salted water to a boil, add the cabbage and apple trimmings, and bring to a boil again to make a broth. Cook for about 30 minutes, then strain the liquid and set it aside. Preheat the oven to 325°F (160°C/Gas mark 3). In a large ovenproof sauté pan, melt the butter over medium heat and sweat the diced apple until tender. Add the sliced cabbage and pour in the brown ale and the broth from the trimmings. Add the thyme and bay leaf. Cover with a lid, transfer to the oven, and cook for 35 minutes. Lift out the cabbage and apples with a slotted spoon and set aside. Place the pan on the stovetop and boil until the juices are reduced and concentrated. Spoon some of the cabbage and apple mixture into the center of each whole cabbage leaf, season with fleur de sel and pepper, tuck in the sides, and roll up into round parcels, using plastic wrap to help give the parcels a neat shape, if you wish. Remove the plastic wrap, if used, butter a large sauté pan, and place the stuffed cabbage parcels in it. Add the braising juices and cook over medium heat for 10 minutes, spooning over the juices to glaze the parcels.

TO SERVE

Wash and core 2 of the apples. Cut each one crosswise into 6 slices just under ½ in. (1 cm) thick. Melt 1½ tablespoons (20 g) butter in a sauté pan and fry the apple slices on both sides until lightly caramelized. Using a melon baller, scoop out tiny balls from the remaining apples. Arrange an apple slice on each plate and place a cabbage parcel and the apple balls on top. Whisk the remaining butter into the braising juices and add a little brown ale at the last moment. Serve with the parcels, spooning it around the apple slices.

KOHLRABI TAGINE WITH DRIED FRUITS

Tajine de choux-raves aux fruits secs

Serves 6

Active time
45 minutes

Cooking time
30 minutes

Equipment
Melon baller
Pestle and mortar

Ingredients

Kohlrabi
6 kohlrabi
1 thyme sprig
1 bay leaf
Fleur de sel

Dried fruits
3 tbsp (50 ml) orange flower water
2/3 cup (3½ oz./100 g) Zante currants
3½ oz. (100 g) dates, pitted

Spice mix
3 garlic cloves
1 bunch scallions
1 tsp ground cumin
1 tsp turmeric
1 tsp coriander seeds
3 whole star anise
½ tsp fenugreek
½ tsp green aniseed
2 saffron threads
½ tsp cubeb (Java) pepper
3 tbsp (50 ml) olive oil

Herbs
1 bunch cilantro
½ bunch mint
1 bunch flat-leaf parsley

To serve
1 lemon

PREPARING THE KOHLRABI

Wash and peel the kohlrabi, keeping their round shape. Cut each one in two horizontally and, using a spoon, remove the flesh from the inside, leaving about ½ in. (1 cm) around the edge. Cut the flesh into small dice and blanch with the thyme and bay leaf in a large saucepan of boiling salted water for 5 minutes. Drain and set aside.

PREPARING THE DRIED FRUITS

In a saucepan, heat ¾ cup (200 ml) water with the orange flower water and bring almost to a boil. Remove from the heat, add the currants and dates and leave to soak to rehydrate them.

PREPARING THE SPICES AND COOKING THE TAGINE

Peel and chop the garlic. Cut the scallions into halfmoon slices (see technique p. 55). Pound all the spices together using a pestle and mortar. Pour the olive oil into a large saucepot over medium heat, add the spices, and roast until fragrant, taking care not to burn them. Add the garlic and scallions and sweat until they soften but do not color. Arrange the kohlrabi halves over the garlic, scallions, and spices. Drain the water used for soaking the dried fruit and pour into the saucepan, reserving the dried fruits. Bring to a simmer over low heat and cook until the kohlrabi halves are tender—the tip of a knife inserted into one should slide in easily—and they are glazed with the cooking liquid.

PREPARING THE HERBS

Pick the cilantro, mint, and parsley leaves from the stems. Wash and chop very finely, rolling them up in paper towel like a cigar (see technique p. 54).

TO SERVE

Peel the lemon, removing all the white pith, and cut the zest into julienne strips (see technique p. 58). Blanch the strips once in boiling water. Place the bottom half of a kohlrabi on each plate, fill with the diced kohlrabi, dried fruits, and juilienned lemon zest, and top with the other kohlrabi half. Scatter over the chopped herbs just before serving.

CHEFS' NOTES

You can use white or purple kohlrabi, as the tajine spice mix complements both of their flavors.

KALE AND CANDIED WALNUT SALAD

Salade de kale et noix confites

Serves 10

Active time
1½ hours

Cooking time
55 minutes

Equipment
Silicone baking mat
Mandoline
Melon baller
Girolle cheese curler

Ingredients

Candied walnuts
Scant ⅓ cup (2 oz./60 g) sugar
¼ cup (60 ml) water
1 cup (3½ oz./100 g) walnut halves

Puffed rice
2 tbsp (1 oz./30 g) steamed long-grain rice

Kale salad
1 bunch baby kale
1 bunch round red radishes
1 Red Delicious apple
2 celery stalks
½ Tête de Moine cheese (see Chefs' Notes)
Salt

Dressing
¼ cup (60 g) plain yogurt
1 tbsp (15 g) wholegrain mustard
1½ tbsp (25 ml) cider vinegar
1½ tbsp (30 g) honey
Scant ½ cup (100 ml) olive oil

To serve
Scant ½ cup (1½ oz./40 g) dried cranberries

PREPARING THE CANDIED WALNUTS

In a heavy saucepan over medium heat, melt the sugar in the water, and then bring to a boil to make a syrup. Add the walnuts, lower the heat to medium, and cook for about 20 minutes to candy them. Drain and spread the walnuts on a silicone baking mat. Preheat the oven to 240°F (120°C/Gas mark ½) and dry out the walnuts in the oven for 35 minutes.

PREPARING THE PUFFED RICE

Add the rice to a dry skillet (with no added fat) and place, uncovered, over high heat until the rice puffs up, shaking the pan occasionally.

PREPARING THE KALE SALAD

Blanch any larger kale leaves in a saucepan of boiling salted water. Wash the radishes and, holding each one by its green top, slice them very finely on the mandoline. Wash the apple and, using a melon baller, scoop out balls of apple flesh (see technique p. 85). Remove the stringy outer layer of the celery stalks with a vegetable peeler and blanch in a saucepan of boiling salted water. Drain, refresh in a bowl of ice water and then cut into angled slices (see technique p. 64). Using a cheese curler, scrape the cheese into frills. Combine all the ingredients in a large bowl.

PREPARING THE DRESSING

Whisk all the ingredients together in a bowl to form an emulsion. Drizzle over the salad and toss to combine.

TO SERVE

Divide the dressed salad between soup plates and sprinkle with the puffed rice, candied walnuts, and cranberries.

CHEFS' NOTES

Tête de Moine (Monk's Head) is a semi-hard Swiss mountain cheese that can be scraped into delicate frills using a girolle cheese curler. If unavailable, fine shavings of any strongly flavored semi-hard cheese can be substituted.

JENNIFER'S KIMCHI
WITH SUNNY SIDE UP EGGS AND OYSTERS

Kimchi de Jennifer, œuf miroir et huîtres

Serves 6

Active time
30 minutes

Marinating time
4–12 hours

Fermentation time
3–4 days

Cooking time
5 minutes

Equipment
3-quart (3-liter) jar
Food processor
Silicone baking mat with a honeycomb pattern
Electric hand beater
1¼-in. (3-cm) round cookie cutter

Ingredients

Brined cabbage
1 head napa cabbage (Chinese leaves)
½ cup (125 g) kosher salt
8 cups (2 liters) water

Kimchi paste
2 tbsp (20 g) glutinous (sticky) rice flour
½ cup (125 ml) water
7¾ oz. (220 g) daikon
2 tbsp (30 g) grated fresh ginger
2 tbsp (25 g) granulated sugar
½ chopped white onion
4 peeled garlic cloves
¾ oz. (25 g) salted fermented shrimp
4 finely chopped scallions
3–6 tbsp (45–90 ml) nuoc mam
¼ cup (60 ml) gochugaru (red chili flakes)
Korean red chili pepper powder, to taste

Honeycomb squid ink tuiles
Scant ½ cup (2 oz./50 g) all-purpose flour
3 tbsp (2 oz./50 g) very soft butter
Scant ¼ cup (1¾ oz./50 g) egg white (about 2 whites)
½ tsp (2.5 ml) squid ink

To serve
18 oysters
6 eggs
Green part of 1 scallion, chopped
1 handful edible red oxalis (wood sorrel)
1 sprig dill
20 borage flowers

PREPARING THE BRINED CABBAGE

Wash the cabbage and cut it lengthwise into 6 or 8 wedges, depending on size. Dissolve the salt in the water to make a brine and pour into a large jar. Add the cabbage wedges and sit a weight on top so they are fully submerged in the brine. Close the jar and marinate at room temperature for 4 hours (or up to 12 hours) until the leaves are softened. Carefully rinse the cabbage under cold running water to remove the salt, drain well, and set aside. Wash and dry the jar.

PREPARING THE KIMCHI PASTE

In a small saucepan, stir the rice flour into the water until dissolved. Bring to a boil, whisking constantly, and cook for 1–2 minutes, until thickened. Remove from the heat and let cool. Peel, wash, and cut the daikon into julienne strips (see technique p. 58). In a food processor, combine the ginger, sugar, white onion, and garlic. Finely chop the shrimp and add with the scallions, nuoc mam, gochugaru, and chili powder. Process until combined, then stir into the rice flour mixture to make a paste. Using your hands, generously coat each cabbage wedge with the paste. Place the wedges on top of each other in the clean jar, close the jar, let ferment for 2 days at room temperature, and then refrigerate. The fermentation will continue naturally and you can serve your kimchi after 3–4 days.

PREPARING THE LACY SQUID INK TUILES

Preheat the oven to 325°F (170°C/Gas mark 3). Place the silicone baking mat on a baking sheet. In a medium bowl, whisk all the ingredients together and spread evenly over the baking mat. Bake for 8 minutes, carefully remove the tuiles from the baking mat, and use the cookie cutter to cut out 18 rounds. Let cool.

TO SERVE

Carefully shuck the oysters. In a non-stick skillet, fry the eggs, remove from the pan, and neatly trim the edges of the white using a large cookie cutter or a sharp knife. Place a large cabbage leaf on each serving plate. Take 3 more leaves, roll them up, and place on the open leaf on each plate, with spaces between them. Arrange the oysters between the cabbage rolls and garnish with the chopped scallion greens, oxalis flowers, small dill sprigs, and borage flowers. Carefully place an egg alongside the cabbage and garnish each plate with 3 squid ink tuiles.

CHEFS' NOTES

Brining is a crucial stage in making kimchi. It helps remove some of the water in the cabbage and promotes lacto-fermentation. A vegetable that has undergone lacto-fermentation will keep for several months in a sealed jar in the refrigerator.

BOK CHOY RAVIOLI WITH CRAB

Ravioles de pak choï et tourteau

Serves 2

Active time
1 hour

Freezing time
3 hours (optional)

Cooking time
30 minutes

Equipment
2¾-in. (7-cm) round cookie cutter
Skimmer
Crab shell cracker
Food processor
Mandoline
Silicone baking mat with a butterfly pattern

Ingredients

Bok choy
1 head bok choy

Stuffing
2 crabs
½ shallot
¼ bunch chervil
A little olive oil
Finely grated zest of 1 small finger of a Buddha's hand fruit
Salt and freshly ground pepper

Miso-citrus mayonnaise
1 egg
3 tbsp (50 ml) sherry vinegar
⅓ oz. (10 g) brown miso paste
Finely grated zest of ¼ small finger of a Buddha's hand fruit
½ cup (120 ml) peanut oil
Fine sea salt

Butterfly tuiles
3 tbsp (2 oz./50 g) very soft butter
Scant ¼ cup (1¾ oz./50 g) lightly beaten egg white (about 2 whites)
Scant ½ cup (2 oz./50 g) all-purpose flour
⅔ oz. (20 g) yellow miso paste

To serve
1 finger of a Buddha's hand fruit
Pieces of crab claw meat

PREPARING THE BOK CHOY
Separate and wash the bok choy leaves. Using the cookie cutter, cut out 6 disks from the green part of the leaves, and set aside the white stems. Blanch the disks for 10 seconds in a saucepan of boiling salted water, drain, and immediately refresh in cold water (see technique p. 88). Pat dry with paper towel.

PREPARING THE STUFFING
Freeze the crabs for 3 hours to numb them before cooking or, if you prefer, ask your fishmonger to kill them for you. Boil the crabs in a little boiling water in a large pot for 5–10 minutes. Lift out of the pan with a skimmer, carefully snap off the large and small claws, and return the bodies to the pan to cook for an additional 5 minutes. Crack the crab shells and remove the meat from the body and claws, taking care to ensure the meat from the large claws remains intact. Peel and chop the shallot, wash and chop the chervil. Weigh out 2 oz. (60 g) of the white bok choy stems and cut into brunoise (see technique p. 60). In a skillet with a little olive oil, sweat the shallot, add the chopped bok choy stems, and cook over low heat until soft. Remove from the heat and let cool. Add most of the crab meat, reserving whole pieces from the large claws, and mix into the shallot and bok choy with the chervil and grated zest from the Buddha's hand fruit. Season with salt and pepper.

PREPARING THE MISO-CITRUS MAYONNAISE
Soft-boil the egg and peel off the shell. In a food processor, combine the egg with the vinegar, miso paste, and salt. Add the grated Buddha's hand fruit zest and then gradually whisk in the oil. Set aside.

PREPARING THE RAVIOLI
Place a little stuffing in each of the bok choy disks and fold over to enclose.

PREPARING THE BUTTERFLY TUILES
Preheat the oven to 325°F (160°C/Gas mark 3). Whisk all the ingredients together until evenly combined. Spread the mixture over the silicone baking mat with a butterfly pattern and bake in the oven for 6 minutes.

TO SERVE
Using the mandoline, cut the Buddha's hand fruit finger into 1/16-in. (1-mm) slices. Spoon a pool of mayonnaise into the center of each serving plate. Arrange alternately the bok choy ravioli, reserved crab claw meat cut into pieces, and Buddha's hand fruit slices around each plate. Garnish with the butterfly tuiles.

LEGUMES

MINTED GARDEN PEAS TWO WAYS, WITH NECTARINES, RASPBERRIES, AND SQUID ROLLS

Déclinaison de petits pois mentholés,
brugnons marbrés de framboises et rouleaux d'encornets

Serves 6

Active time
2 hours

Cooking time
30 minutes

Equipment
Blender
Fine-mesh sieve
Sous vide bags
Steam oven or steamer
Thermometer

Ingredients

Minted pea puree
4½ lb. (2 kg) fresh garden peas in their pods
1 cup (250 ml) grapeseed oil
3 tbsp (50 ml) cream, minimum 35% fat
2 drops mint essential oil

Garnishes
2 nectarines
3 tuberous chervil
3½ oz. (100 g) raspberries
1²/₃ cups (400 ml) grapeseed oil, divided
Fine sea salt

Squid rolls
6 whole squid
2 oz. (60 g) lard
¾ cup plus 2 tbsp (3½ oz./100 g) all-purpose flour
Oil for frying

To serve
12 pea shoots
3 marigolds
6–12 fresh raspberries

PREPARING THE MINTED PEA PUREE

Shell the peas (see technique p. 48), reserving the pods. Bring a saucepan of boiling salted water to a boil, blanch the pods, and drain well. Place the pods in a blender, add the grapeseed oil, and blend until smooth. Do this in batches, if necessary, adding some of the oil each time. Strain through a fine-mesh sieve, reserving the oil. In a saucepan, boil the peas *à l'anglaise* and then refresh them in a bowl of ice water (see technique p. 90). Using a blender (or immersion blender), process half the peas with the cream to obtain a puree and strain through a fine-mesh sieve. Season the remaining peas with the mint essential oil and the reserved oil from straining the pea pod puree.

PREPARING THE GARNISHES

Peel, pit, and cut the nectarines into quarters. Peel the tuberous chervil and cut into quarters as well. Crush the raspberries. Place the nectarines and tuberous chervil in separate sous vide bags with half the crushed raspberries in each, half the grapeseed oil, and a pinch of salt. Seal and cook in a steam oven at 203°F (95°C) or a steamer, allowing 5 minutes for the nectarines and 15 minutes for the tuberous chervil.

PREPARING THE SQUID ROLLS

Separate the squid bodies from the tentacles, remove the quills, and trim. Set aside the tentacles. Place the bodies flat on a board and cut open lengthwise. Score the squid bodies in a crisscross pattern with a sharp knife. Melt the lard in a large skillet and sauté the bodies, which will curl as they fry. Heat an oil bath to 350°F (180°C). Roll the tentacles in the flour and place them in the hot oil. Deep-fry until golden and drain on paper towel.

TO SERVE

Spoon the pea puree into the center of each serving plate and the minted peas over it. Arrange the nectarines, tuberous chervil, and squid attractively on the plates and garnish with the pea shoots, marigold petals, and raspberries.

FAVA BEAN FALAFEL AND GRILLED HALLOUMI

Falafels de fèves et halloumi grillé

Serves 6

Active time
30 minutes

Cooking time
15 minutes

Resting time
20 minutes

Equipment
Food processor
Thermometer
Pot with deep-frying basket or deep fryer
Skimmer
Grill pan

Ingredients

Falafel
14 oz. (400 g) fresh fava beans
1 scallion
3 garlic cloves
1 bunch flat-leaf parsley
1 bunch cilantro
3 tbsp (50 ml) water, or more if needed
1 tbsp (15 g) ground cumin
1 tbsp (15 g) ground coriander
2 tbsp (20 g) golden sesame seeds
1 tsp (5 g) baking powder
A little flour, if needed
Salt and pepper
Oil for deep-frying

Tzatziki
1 cucumber
1 garlic clove
10 mint leaves
14 oz. (400 g) Greek yogurt
Juice of ½ lemon
Olive oil
Salt and freshly ground pepper

Grilled halloumi
18 slices halloumi
Olive oil
3 oregano sprigs, leaves finely chopped

To serve
Olive oil
2 oz. (50 g) cooked fresh fava beans
18 thin slices Persian cucumber
Red chili pepper, finely sliced
Piment d'Espelette

PREPARING THE FALAFEL

Shell the fava beans (see technique p. 48), blanch them briefly in a saucepan of boiling salted water, refresh in a bowl of ice water, and then peel off the skins. Peel and roughly chop the scallion and garlic. Wash and chop the parsley and cilantro (see technique p. 54). In a food processor, combine the scallion, garlic, parsley, and cilantro. Add the fava beans and process briefly to a fairly rough texture, adding water to soften it, as necessary. Season with the cumin, coriander, sesame seeds, salt, and pepper and mix in the baking powder. Check the texture of the mixture by frying a small piece in hot oil. If it still seems dry, add a little water. If too soft, stir in a little flour. Using your hands, shape the falafel mixture into 1½-in. (4-cm) patties, ¾ in. (2 cm) thick. Heat the oil for deep-frying to 350°F (180°C) and lower the falafel into the oil using the basket or a skimmer. Fry until golden on all sides. Remove from the oil and drain on paper towel. Season with salt.

PREPARING THE TZATZIKI

Peel and grate the cucumber. Place it in a bowl, sprinkle with salt, and let rest for 20 minutes. Peel and crush the garlic to a paste. Wash and chop the mint leaves. Squeeze the cucumber between your hands to remove excess water, rinse, and combine with the yogurt, garlic, lemon juice, mint, and a little olive oil. Season with salt and pepper and set aside in the refrigerator.

PREPARING THE GRILLED HALLOUMI

Grease a grill pan with a little olive oil and, when very hot, grill the halloumi slices, turning them over once. Sprinkle over the oregano.

TO SERVE

Arrange 3 small mounds of tzatziki drizzled with olive oil, 3 slices of grilled halloumi, and 3 falafels attractively on each plate. Garnish with a few cooked fava beans, slices of Persian cucumber and red chili pepper, and a dusting of piment d'Espelette.

CREAMED SNOW PEA QUENELLES AND WHITING LOGS

Royale de pois gourmands, godiveaux de merlan

Serves 6

Active time
1 hour

Freezing time
30 minutes

Cooking time
1 hour

Equipment
Food processor
12 cavity silicone quenelle mold or other shape of your choice
Steam oven or steamer
Immersion blender
Fine-mesh sieve

Ingredients

Creamed snow pea quenelles
6 oz. (180 g) snow peas
¾ tsp (4 g) sea salt
1 whole egg
2 egg yolks
3 tbsp (50 ml) cream, minimum 35% fat
Salt and freshly ground pepper

Arugula cream
2 oz. (50 g) arugula
Scant ½ cup (100 ml) vegetable stock
Scant ½ cup (100 ml) cream, minimum 35% fat
Salt and freshly ground pepper

Whiting logs
9 oz. (250 g) skinned whiting fillet
2 tbsp (1 oz./30 g) butter, softened
2 tsp (⅓ oz./10 g) egg white (about ⅓ white)
½ cup (125 ml) cream, minimum 35% fat
Salt and freshly ground pepper

Snow peas
14 oz. (400 g) snow peas

To serve
7 oz. (200 g) cockles
¾ oz. (20 g) avruga
18 tarragon leaves

PREPARING THE CREAMED SNOW PEA QUENELLES

In a saucepan of well-salted boiling water, cook the snow peas until very tender. Refresh them in a bowl of ice water. Place in a food processor, blend to a puree, and then strain. Weigh out 5 oz. (150 g) of the puree and stir in the egg, egg yolks, and cream. Season with salt and pepper. Pour the mixture into the molds and cook in a steam oven at 167°F (75°C) or in a steamer for 35 minutes. Let cool, then freeze for 30 minutes so the quenelles can be easily unmolded.

PREPARING THE ARUGULA CREAM

In a saucepan of boiling salted water, blanch the arugula for 30 seconds, and then refresh in a bowl of ice water. Drain well. Using an immersion blender, process with the vegetable stock and cream. Transfer to a saucepan over low heat and simmer for 5 minutes to reduce. Strain through a fine-mesh sieve. Season with salt and pepper and check the consistency is creamy enough to coat the back of a spoon. If not, return the cream to the saucepan and reduce a little more.

PREPARING THE WHITING LOGS

Grind the whiting in a food processor, incorporate the butter, and then the egg white. Strain through a fine-mesh sieve into a bowl set over a larger bowl half-filled with ice cubes. Using a flexible spatula, stir in the cream and season with salt and pepper. Cut 6 sheets of plastic wrap, divide the mixture between them, and roll up tightly into cylinders. Cook in a steam oven at 185°F (85°C) or in a steamer for 8–10 minutes. Cool and then refrigerate until ready to serve.

PREPARING THE SNOW PEAS

Boil the snow peas *à l'anglaise* (see technique p. 90) in a large saucepan of salted boiling water, and then drain. Arrange several snow peas side by side, overlapping them slightly, and cut them into 6 rectangles measuring 6 × 2½ in. (15 × 6 cm). Line a baking sheet with parchment paper and carefully lift and place the rectangles on it.

TO SERVE

Clean and open the cockles in a steamer or oven at 185°F (85°C/Gas at lowest possible temperature) for 3 minutes. Unwrap and cut each cylinder of whiting into 3 log shapes. Reheat the whiting logs, snow pea rectangles, and snow pea quenelles in a steam oven or steamer for a few minutes. Coat the snow pea quenelles with the arugula cream. Place a snow pea rectangle on each serving plate and arrange 3 quenelles, 3 whiting logs, a few cockles, and a little avruga on top. Garnish with the tarragon leaves. Pipe any remaining arugula cream in dots alongside.

GREEN BEAN SALAD WITH SHALLOTS AND HAZELNUTS

Salade de haricots verts, échalotes et noisettes du Piémont

Serves 6

Active time
30 minutes

Soaking time
20 minutes

Cooking time
10 minutes

Ingredients

Bean salad

2 lb. 10 oz. (1.2 kg) green beans (or half green and half yellow wax beans)

4 cups (1 liter) high-sodium sparkling water

1½ oz. (40 g) sea salt

2 large shallots

Scant 1 cup (5 oz./150 g) hazelnuts

2 bunches chives

Vinaigrette

3 tbsp (50 ml) Barolo vinegar

Scant 1 cup (100 ml) hazelnut oil

Fleur de sel

Freshly ground pepper

PREPARING THE BEAN SALAD

Trim the beans (see technique p. 49), wash in cold water, and then soak them in the sparkling water for 20 minutes, as this will make the beans more tender and set their color. Drain. Bring a saucepan of water to a boil. Add the salt, cook the beans *à l'anglaise* so they retain their crunch (see technique p. 90), and refresh in a bowl of ice water. Peel the shallots, slice into rounds, and separate into rings. Rinse under cold water. Preheat the oven to 250°F (120°C/Gas mark ½). Line a baking sheet with parchment paper, spread the hazelnuts over it, and toast for 5–8 minutes, until golden. Remove from the baking sheet and, when cool enough to handle, roughly chop. Wash and finely chop or snip the chives (see Chefs' Notes p. 54).

PREPARING THE VINAIGRETTE

Whisk the vinegar and hazelnut oil together in a bowl and season with a little fleur de sel and freshly ground pepper.

TO SERVE

Toss the beans with the vinaigrette and scatter over the shallots, chopped hazelnuts, and chopped chives.

PAIMPOL HARICOT BEAN STEW WITH RAZOR CLAMS AND MUSHROOMS

Ragoût de cocos de Paimpol, coquillages et champignons

Serves 6

Active time
40 minutes

Cooking time
40 minutes

Ingredients

Haricot beans and mushrooms

4½ lb. (2 kg) fresh white haricot beans (cocos de Paimpol)

1 lb. (500 g) button mushrooms

7 oz. (200 g) girolle mushrooms

2 shallots

7 tbsp (3½ oz./100 g) butter

Razor clam marinière sauce

2¼ lb. (1 kg) razor clams

1 small shallot

¾ cup (200 ml) white wine

Stew

4 cups (1 liter) vegetable stock

½ oz. (15 g) chorizo

Salt and freshly ground pepper

To serve

1 bunch basil

1 bunch chives

Croutons (optional)

PREPARING THE HARICOT BEANS AND MUSHROOMS

Shell the haricot beans (see technique p. 48) and set aside. Prepare and clean both types of mushroom (see technique p. 35). Cut the mushrooms into ¼-in. (5-mm) macedoine (see technique p. 65) and peel and chop the shallots (see technique p. 56). Melt the butter in a large skillet over high heat and sauté the mushrooms with the shallots.

PREPARING THE RAZOR CLAM MARINIÈRE SAUCE

Wash and open the razor clams. Peel and chop the shallot. Place the razor clams and shallot in a saucepot over medium-high heat, pour in the wine, and cover. Cook for 3-4 minutes, or until the shells have opened. Remove the clams from their shells and finely dice.

PREPARING THE STEW

Cook the haricot beans in the vegetable stock for 20 minutes. Cut the chorizo into brunoise (see technique p. 60) and sweat in a small skillet so it renders its fat. Season the haricot beans with salt and pepper and add the mushrooms, chorizo, and diced clams.

TO SERVE

Wash and chop the basil and chop or snip the chives (see Chefs' Notes p. 54). Heat serving dishes and divide the stew between them. Scatter over the chopped herbs and add croutons, if wished.

CHEFS' NOTES

The coco de Paimpol is a PDO (Protected Designation of Origin) shelling bean from Brittany that is sold in fresh or semi-dried form. If you can't find this variety, substitute dried white beans, such as navy beans, and adapt the cooking time according to package instructions.

MUSHROOMS

CRISP AND CREAMY BUTTON MUSHROOM AND COFFEE ROULADE

Dessert moelleux et croustillant autour du café et du champignon de Paris

Serves 10

Active time
2 hours

Drying time
Overnight

Cooking time
2 hours

Equipment
Silicone baking mat
Electric hand beater
Thermometer
Food processor
Stand mixer
2 pastry bags, 1 fitted with a plain ¼-in. (4–5-mm) tip

Ingredients

Dried mushroom powder
5 oz. (150 g) button mushrooms

Coffee sponge cake layer
1⅔ cups (7 oz./190 g) all-purpose flour
¾ tsp (3 g) baking powder
12 oz. (350 g) eggs (about 7 eggs)
1¼ cups (9 oz./250 g) granulated sugar
2 tbsp (30 ml) water
1½ tsp (7 ml) caramel syrup
A few drops of coffee extract
1½ tbsp (6 g) instant coffee
Confectioners' sugar for dusting

Coffee imbibing syrup
2 tsp (8 g) granulated sugar
⅔ cup (150 ml) hot espresso coffee

Coffee butter cream
Italian meringue
⅓ cup (80 ml) water
¾ cup (5 oz./145 g) superfine sugar
⅓ cup (2½ oz./75 g) egg white (about 2½ whites)

Pouring custard
Scant ½ cup (115 ml) reduced fat milk
⅓ cup (3 oz./90 g) egg yolks (about 4½ yolks)
½ cup plus 2 tbsp (4 oz./115 g) granulated sugar
4½ sticks (1 lb. 2 oz./500 g) unsalted butter, diced, at room temperature
Coffee extract to taste

Hazelnut meringue
½ cup (2¼ oz./65 g) confectioners' sugar
1 cup minus 2½ tbsp (6¾ oz./190 g) superfine sugar, divided
¾ cup (2¼ oz./65 g) ground hazelnuts
½ cup (4½ oz. 125 g) egg white (about 4 whites)

Hazelnut cream
2 sheets gelatin
9 oz. (250 g) pastry cream
5 oz. (150 g) hazelnut praline
Scant ½ cup (100 ml) cream, minimum 35% fat

To serve
5-7 button mushrooms

PREPARING THE DRIED MUSHROOM POWDER

A day ahead, clean and finely chop the button mushrooms (see technique p. 75). Dry them out overnight in a 140°F (60°C/Gas on lowest setting) oven. Grind to a powder.

PREPARING THE COFFEE SPONGE CAKE LAYER

Preheat the oven to 475°F (240°C/Gas mark 9). Line a baking sheet with a silicone baking mat. Sift the flour with the baking powder. Using an electric hand beater, beat the eggs with the sugar until pale and thick. Beat in the water, caramel syrup, coffee extract, and instant coffee. Fold in the flour and baking powder until fully incorporated and spread the batter in a thin layer over the baking sheet. Bake for 2 minutes in the oven, remove, immediately dust with confectioners' sugar, and let cool. To make the imbibing syrup, dissolve the sugar in the hot espresso, then let cool. Brush the syrup over the cooled sponge.

PREPARING THE BUTTER CREAM

To make the Italian meringue, heat the water with the sugar until the sugar dissolves, bring to a boil and continue boiling until the temperature reaches 244°F (118°C). In the meantime, in a stand mixer fitted with the whisk, whisk the egg whites until they hold firm peaks. Whisk in the syrup in a steady drizzle, whisking until the meringue cools to room temperature. To make the pouring custard, bring the milk to a boil in a medium saucepan. In a large mixing bowl, whisk the egg yolks with the sugar until pale and thick. Whisk a little of the hot milk into the yolk and sugar mixture, pour it back into the saucepan, and place back over the heat, stirring constantly, until the temperature of the custard reaches 183°F (84°C). Let the custard cool slightly, pour it over the butter, and, using an electric hand beater, whisk until foamy. Using a flexible spatula, fold in the Italian meringue and flavor with the coffee extract.

PREPARING THE HAZELNUT MERINGUE

Preheat the oven to 265°F (130°C/Gas mark 1). Line a baking sheet with a silicone baking mat. In a food processor, very finely grind the confectioners' sugar with a scant ⅓ cup (2¼ oz./65 g) of the superfine sugar and the ground hazelnuts. In a stand mixer fitted with the whisk, whisk the egg whites, gradually adding the remaining ⅔ cup (4½ oz./125 g) superfine sugar, until the mixture holds firm peaks. Using a flexible spatula, fold in the dry ingredients. Transfer to the pastry bag fitted with a plain ¼-in. (4–5-mm) tip and pipe long log shapes on the baking sheet. Dry out in the oven for 2 hours or until crisp. Let cool, then crush into small pieces.

PREPARING THE HAZELNUT CREAM

Soak the gelatin in a bowl of cold water until softened. In a saucepan over low heat, warm the pastry cream with the hazelnut praline. Squeeze the excess water from the gelatin and stir in until dissolved. Let cool. Whip the cream until it holds soft peaks and lightly fold in.

TO ASSEMBLE AND SERVE

Spread some of the butter cream over the sponge layer. Finely slice the raw button mushrooms and dot them over the butter cream, setting aside a few slices for decoration. Roll up the sponge into a tight, thin cylinder, cover with the remaining butter cream, and roll in the crushed meringue until coated. Cut into ¾-in. (2-cm) slices. Brush hazelnut cream over each serving plate. Spoon the remaining cream into a pastry bag, snip off the tip, and pipe small mounds on top. Arrange 2 roulade slices on each plate, along with a few mushroom slices, and dust lightly with the dried mushroom powder.

GIROLLE CRÉMEUX WITH STEAMED EGGS

Crémeux de girolles et œuf parfait

Serves 6

Active time
15 minutes

Cooking time
1 hour

Equipment
Steam oven or steamer
Immersion blender
Fine-mesh sieve
2¼-in. (6-cm) round cookie cutter
Water bath
Skimmer

Ingredients

Steamed eggs
6 large eggs in their shells, preferably organic

Girolle crémeux
14 oz. (400 g) girolle mushrooms
1 shallot
3 tbsp (2 oz./60 g) duck fat
¾ cup (200 ml) white chicken stock
¾ cup (200 ml) cream, minimum 35% fat
Salt and freshly ground pepper

To garnish and serve
7 oz. (200 g) girolle mushrooms
1 smoked duck breast
Duck fat for frying
6 slices from a sandwich loaf
1 bunch chives
Vinegar
¼ cup (2 oz./50 g) hazelnuts, halved
A few sprigs of red shiso and red-veined cress

PREPARING THE STEAMED EGGS

Cook the eggs in a steam oven at 145°F (63°C) or steamer for 1 hour.

PREPARING THE GIROLLE CRÉMEUX

While the eggs are steaming, clean and wash the girolle mushrooms (see technique p. 35), including those for garnish. Peel and chop the shallot (see technique p. 56). Melt the duck fat in a medium saucepan over medium heat and sweat the shallot for a few minutes without letting it color. Add the 14 oz. (400 g) girolle mushrooms, sweat for several minutes, and then pour in the chicken stock. Bring to a simmer, reduce the heat to low, and simmer for about 10 minutes. Blend until smooth using an immersion blender and then strain through a fine-mesh sieve. Stir in the cream and bring to a boil again. Remove from the heat, season with salt and pepper, and set aside.

TO GARNISH AND SERVE

Finely slice the smoked duck breast. Melt the duck fat in a hot skillet and briefly sauté the girolle mushrooms. Remove from the skillet but keep the duck fat. Using the cookie cutter, cut out 6 disks of bread and fry them in the duck fat until golden brown. Wash and finely chop or snip the chives. Reheat the girolle mushroom crémeux. When the eggs are almost ready, heat a water bath with a good dash of vinegar added to a simmer. Carefully crack the eggs into the hot water to complete the coagulation process: the whites should be set but the yolks still runny. Lift out the eggs carefully using a skimmer. Pour the girolle mushroom crémeux into soup plates, place a disk of fried bread in the center, and top with an egg. Roll up the slices of duck breast and arrange them around with the sautéed girolles, chopped chives, hazelnut halves, and small sprigs of red shiso and red-veined cress.

PORCINI TARTLETS WITH GARLIC AND CHIVE WHIPPED CREAM

Tartelettes aux cèpes, chantilly ail et ciboulette

Serves 4

Active time
1 hour

Resting time
30 minutes

Chilling time
1 hour 10 minutes

Cooking time
1 hour

Equipment
4 × 2½-in. (8-cm) tartlet rings
Silicone baking mat
Electric hand beater
Paper piping cone

Ingredients

Tart crust
2 cups (9 oz./250 g) all-purpose flour
1 stick plus 2 tsp (4½ oz./125 g) unsalted butter, chilled
4 tbsp (60 ml) cold water
1 tsp (5 g) salt
1 egg yolk
¾ oz. (20 g) activated charcoal powder

Porcini-celery root filling
5 oz. (150 g) celery root
A little lemon juice or vinegar
3½ oz. (100 g) foie gras (optional)
1 lb. 5 oz. (600 g) porcini
1 oz. (30 g) shallot (about 1 medium shallot)
2 tsp (10 g) butter
Scant ½ cup (100 ml) white chicken stock
1 tsp chopped parsley
Salt and freshly ground pepper

Porcini topping
14 oz. (400 g) porcini
Clarified butter for frying

Garlic and chive whipped cream
½ bunch chives
1⅔ cups (400 ml) cream, minimum 35% fat
2 oz. (50 g) garlic puree
Salt and freshly ground pepper

To serve
4 small (button) porcini
Clarified butter for frying
⅔ cup (150 ml) thick cream, diluted to a piping consistency with a little water
1 tsp (3 g) poppy seeds
Small sprigs of salad burnet and red shiso
2 tbsp fried onions
A little porcini powder

PREPARING THE TART CRUST

Sift the flour onto a clean work surface. Dice the butter and rub it into the flour until the mixture looks like bread crumbs. Make a well in the center and add the water, salt, and egg yolk. Using a dough scraper, bring the ingredients together, and then knead gently with your hands to form a dough. Weigh out one-third of the dough and knead the activated charcoal into it. Shape each piece of dough into a ball, flatten slightly, cover with plastic wrap, and let rest in the refrigerator for 30 minutes, so the doughs are no longer elastic. Working with one ball of dough at a time, roll out between two sheets of parchment paper to a thickness of ¼ in. (5 mm). Place the tartlet rings on a silicone baking mat. Cut out 4 × 2½-in. (8-cm) disks of plain dough, place them in the tartlet rings, and chill for 20 minutes in the refrigerator. Cut each of the 2 doughs into long strips measuring ½ in. (1 cm) in width. Using a brush, dampen the long edges of the strips with water and press a strip of each of the 2 doughs together to seal firmly and make 1 wide 2-color strip. Cut the strips so they fit the inside wall of each ring. Dampen the disks of dough lining the bottom of the tartlet rings and fit a strip into each ring (with the charcoal dough at the top), pressing firmly to seal it tightly to the base. Trim away excess dough. Chill in the refrigerator for 20 minutes so the dough forms a slight crust. Preheat the oven to 325°F (160°C/Gas mark 3) and blind-bake the tartlet cases for 15 minutes. Keep the oven switched on.

PREPARING THE PORCINI-CELERY ROOT FILLING

Wash and peel the celery root, cut into brunoise (see technique p. 60), and place in a bowl of cold water with a squeeze of lemon juice or a little vinegar added to prevent discoloration. In a dry skillet over high heat, briefly sauté the foie gras, if using, without adding any fat. Remove from the pan, pat the foie gras with paper towel to remove excess fat, and cut into brunoise. Clean the porcini (see technique p. 35) and also cut into brunoise. Peel and finely chop the shallot (see technique p. 56). In a sauté pan or deep skillet, sauté the porcini in half the butter. Remove from the pan and set aside. Drain the celery root and pat dry with paper towel. Add the remaining butter to the pan and sweat the shallots and celery root for a few minutes, until the shallot is translucent. Pour in the chicken stock and cook until the celery root is just al dente. Stir in the chopped parsley, the foie gras, and season with salt and pepper. Return the porcini to the pan, stirring to combine all the ingredients. Keep hot.

PREPARING THE PORCINI TOPPING

Clean and slice the porcini. Cook them briefly over high heat in clarified butter, without allowing them to color.

PREPARING THE GARLIC AND CHIVE WHIPPED CREAM

Wash and finely chop or snip the chives (see Chefs' Notes p. 54). Whip the cream until it holds soft peaks. Stir in the garlic puree, chives, salt, and pepper until combined.

TO ASSEMBLE AND SERVE

Spoon the hot porcini-celery root filling into the tartlet cases and arrange the sliced porcini in neat overlapping rows on top. Return to the oven at 325°F (160°C/Gas mark 3) for 5 minutes to reheat. Quarter the small porcini and fry in a little clarified butter until golden. Spoon the cream into a paper piping cone, snip off the tip, and pipe the cream in a spiral on each serving plate. Scatter the poppy seeds over the cream. Carefully place a tartlet and arrange a quartered porcini on each plate. Add a quenelle of garlic and chive whipped cream and garnish with small sprigs of salad burnet and red shiso, fried onions, and a dusting of porcini powder.

FLAT CHANTERELLE OMELET

Omelette plate aux chanterelles

Serves 4

Preparation
20 minutes

Cooking time
10 minutes

Equipment
Pot with deep-frying basket or deep fryer
Thermometer

Ingredients

Toppings
1 shallot
14 oz. (400 g) chanterelle mushrooms
3 tbsp (2 oz./50 g) unsalted butter
1 tbsp chopped fresh parsley
3½ oz. (100 g) confit duck giblets
3½ oz. (100 g) Comté, or other hard cheese with a nutty flavor
3½ oz. (100 g) pearl onions
Scant ½ cup (100 ml) milk
¾ cup plus 2 tbsp (3½ oz./100 g) all-purpose flour
Oil for frying
Salt

Wafers
⅔ cup (160 ml) white chicken stock
2 tbsp (20 g) all-purpose flour
¼ cup (60 ml) rapeseed oil
1 pinch of salt

Omelet
12 eggs
Salt and pepper

To serve
2 scallions
2 oz. (50 g) wild arugula, or arugula
Olive oil for drizzling

PREPARING THE TOPPINGS

Peel and finely chop the shallot (see technique p. 56) and clean the chanterelles (see technique p. 35). In a skillet over high heat, melt the butter and sauté the chanterelles with the shallot. When cooked, stir in the chopped parsley, and keep warm. Cut the giblets into even-sized pieces, melt the fat from their jar in a skillet, add the giblets, and heat through. Remove from the pan and keep warm. Cut the cheese into even-sized dice and set aside. Slice the pearl onions and separate into rings. Pour the milk into a small bowl and spread the flour on a plate. Dip the onion rings in the milk and then in the flour until coated. Fry in an oil bath heated to 325°F (160°C) until golden. Drain on a plate lined with paper towel, season with salt, and keep warm without covering.

PREPARING THE WAFERS

In a medium mixing bowl, combine all the ingredients. Heat a non-stick skillet over high heat, pour in 3 tablespoons of the batter, and cook until lightly colored and crisp. Remove from the pan and repeat, until all the remaining batter has been used.

PREPARING THE OMELET

Beat the eggs and season with salt and pepper. In a skillet over medium heat, add some of the chanterelles and warm through. Pour in the eggs and cook just until they are almost set but still a little runny. Dot the omelet with the diced cheese, giblets, and remaining chanterelles.

TO SERVE

Chop the green tops of the scallions and arrange attractively over the omelet with the fried onion rings and the wild arugula leaves drizzled with a little olive oil. Break the wafers into shards and scatter over the omelet.

SEA URCHIN AND OYSTER MUSHROOM CAPPUCCINO

Cappuccino iodé d'oursin et pleurote

Serves 10

Active time
1 hour

Cooking time
10 minutes

Equipment
Scissors with sharp-pointed blades
Blender
Fine-mesh sieve
Siphon + 2 cartridges

Ingredients

Sea urchins
30 sea urchins

Oyster mushroom foam
2¼ lb. (1 kg) oyster mushrooms (preferably grown on coffee grounds)
Olive oil
2 cups (500 ml) cream, minimum 35% fat
4 tsp (20 ml) espresso coffee
Salt and freshly ground pepper

To serve
Oil for warming the sea urchins
1 cup (5 oz./150 g) roasted unsalted peanuts, roughly chopped
Grated coffee beans

PREPARING THE SEA URCHINS

Using scissors with sharp-pointed blades, cut open the sea urchin shells about one-third from the top, starting at the mouth. Remove the coiled digestive system and discard, then extract the tongues and refrigerate them. Wash the inside of the shells thoroughly and place them upside down on sheets of paper towel to drain.

PREPARING THE OYSTER MUSHROOM FOAM

Clean the oyster mushrooms (see technique p. 35) and slice them. Place a skillet over high heat and, when very hot, add a little olive oil and sauté the mushrooms. Remove half from the skillet and set aside for serving. Deglaze the remaining mushrooms with the cream, scraping the skillet to incorporate any bits sticking to it. Reduce the heat to low and cook until reduced and thickened. Transfer the cream and mushrooms to a blender, process until smooth, and then strain through a fine-mesh sieve. Add the coffee and season with salt and pepper. Pour into the siphon, add the cartridges, and reserve at room temperature.

TO SERVE

Just before serving, gently warm the sea urchin tongues in a skillet with a little olive oil. Return them to their shells and fill with the reserved sautéed mushrooms and the chopped peanuts. Top with the oyster mushroom foam and sprinkle with grated coffee beans.

BRAISED SHIITAKE MUSHROOMS

Shiitakés braisés

Serves 6

Active time
30 minutes

Cooking time
40 minutes

Equipment
1½-in. (4-cm) round cookie cutter

Ingredients
18 large shiitake mushrooms

Shiitake and ham stuffing
1 lb. 5 oz. (600 g) shiitake mushrooms
5 oz. (150 g) shallots
5 slices cured ham
Leaves of 1 bunch tarragon
2 bunches scallions
¾ cup (3½ oz./100 g) pine nuts
3 tbsp (2 oz./50 g) butter
Scant ½ cup (100 ml) dry white wine
1 egg
3 tbsp (50 ml) brown chicken *jus*
Fleur de sel
Freshly ground pepper

To serve
3 tbsp (2 oz./50 g) butter
Oregano sprigs
Yellow frisée lettuce sprigs
1¼ cups (300 ml) chicken *jus*

PREPARING THE SHIITAKE MUSHROOMS
Wash the large shiitake mushrooms and blanch in a saucepan of boiling water for 30 seconds. Drain and set aside.

PREPARING THE SHIITAKE AND HAM STUFFING
Preheat the oven to 300°F (150°C/Gas mark 2). Wash and cut the shiitake mushrooms into brunoise (see technique p. 60). Peel and finely chop the shallots. Finely dice the ham. Wash and chop the tarragon leaves. Wash and slice the scallions. Line a baking sheet with parchment paper and spread the pine nuts over it. Toast in the oven for about 10 minutes, until lightly colored. In a skillet over medium heat, melt the butter and sweat the shallot. Add the shiitake mushrooms, season with salt and pepper, and deglaze with the white wine. Cover and cook for 15 minutes. Transfer to a mixing bowl and combine with the pine nuts, egg, tarragon, scallions, and ham. Season with salt and pepper and stir in the chicken *jus*.

TO SERVE
Using the cookie cutter, cut a disk out of each large shiitake mushroom, then cut each disk crosswise into two. Heat the butter in a skillet and sauté the mushroom disks for 5-10 minutes, until tender. Drain and spoon the stuffing onto half the mushroom disks, placing the remaining disks on top to sandwich the stuffing. Place 3 on each plate and garnish with sprigs of oregano and frisée lettuce. Warm the chicken *jus* and drizzle it over.

PÂTÉ EN CROÛTE WITH BLACK CHANTERELLES

Pâté en croûte aux trompettes-de-la-mort

Serves 8

Active time
3 hours

Marinating and resting time
1 day

Cooking time
5 hours

Equipment
Stand mixer
Meat grinder
Skimmer
14- × 3-in. (35- × 7.5-cm) loaf pan, 3 in. (8 cm) deep
Instant-read thermometer

Ingredients

Pickled black chanterelles
14 oz. (400 g) black chanterelles
2 garlic cloves
1 tbsp (20 g) maple syrup
4 tsp (20 ml) mushroom soy sauce
2 tbsp (30 ml) sherry vinegar
¼ bunch chives
1 tbsp chopped fresh tarragon

Pastry crust
3 sticks (12 oz./350 g) butter
2 tsp (10 g) fine salt
4 tsp (¾ oz./20 g) sugar
5 cups (1 lb. 2 oz./500 g) all-purpose flour
Generous ¼ cup (2 oz./65 g) lightly beaten egg (about 1 egg)
⅓ cup (85 ml) water

Stuffing and meat strips
1 duck
1 grain-fed chicken
1 pigeon
7 oz. (200 g) foie gras (optional)
14 oz. (400 g) pork back fat
14 oz. (400 g) pork neck fillet or collar
3 tbsp (50 ml) white wine
Fine salt and freshly ground pepper

Black chanterelles
1 lb. (500 g) black chanterelles
3 tbsp (2 oz./50 g) unsalted butter

Chicken aspic
Duck, chicken, and pigeon carcasses
1 bouquet garni (leek greens, celery stalk, thyme, bay leaf, and parsley stalk, tied together with kitchen twine)
1 carrot
1 onion
1 leek
3½ oz. (100 g) egg white (about 3 whites)
9 sheets (18 g) gold bloom gelatin

To assemble
Butter for greasing the loaf pan
1 egg yolk
4 tsp (20 ml) water

To serve
Yellow frisée lettuce sprigs
Pea shoots
Hazelnuts

PREPARING THE PICKLED BLACK CHANTERELLES

Clean the mushrooms (see technique p. 35), blanch them briefly in a saucepan of boiling water, and drain. Peel and crush the garlic. In a small saucepan, heat the maple syrup, mushroom soy sauce, vinegar, and garlic and bring to a boil. Pour over the mushrooms, let cool, and then let marinate for 24 hours in the refrigerator. The next day, chop or snip the chives (see Chefs' Notes p. 54) and add along with the chopped tarragon.

PREPARING THE PASTRY CRUST

In the bowl of a stand mixer fitted with the paddle beater, place the butter, salt, sugar, and flour. Add the eggs and water and beat until a smooth dough is obtained. Shape into a ball, cover in plastic wrap, and chill in the refrigerator until needed.

PREPARING THE STUFFING

Bone the duck, chicken, and pigeon, setting the breast and thigh meat to one side and reserving the wings and carcasses for the aspic. Weigh all the meats. Using 2 teaspoons (10 g) of fine salt and 2 teaspoons (5 g) ground pepper for every 2¼ lb. (1 kg) of meat, season the poultry, foie gras, back fat, and pork neck by sprinkling a little salt and pepper over each. Set aside the poultry breasts and foie gras. Cut the remaining meat into chunks, place in a bowl, and add the white wine. Grind the poultry thighs, back fat, and pork neck fillet. Cut the breasts lengthwise into strips just under ½ in. (1 cm) wide and the foie gras into strips of the same size.

PREPARING THE BLACK CHANTERELLES

Clean the mushrooms (see technique p. 35). In a skillet over high heat, sauté them in the butter. Drain and chop finely, cool, and stir into the stuffing. Chill in the refrigerator until assembling.

PREPARING THE CHICKEN ASPIC

Place the poultry carcasses in a large pot of water, add the bouquet garni, and bring slowly to a boil, skimming as necessary. Lower the heat and simmer for 4 hours. Let cool and then refrigerate until the fat has solidified on the surface and the stock is well chilled. Lift off the fat. Peel the carrot and onion and wash the leek (see technique p. 33). Cut the vegetables into brunoise (see technique p. 60). Whisk the egg whites until frothy. Fold the vegetables into the egg whites and stir into the chilled stock. Strain the stock through a clean dish cloth to clarify. Return to a low heat. Soak the gelatin in a bowl of cold water until softened. Squeeze the excess water from the gelatin and stir into the hot stock until melted.

TO ASSEMBLE

Preheat the oven to 425°F (220°C/Gas mark 7). Using a rolling pin, roll out the pastry to a thickness of 1/16–1/8 in. (2–3 mm). Cut it into strips to line the loaf pan and another strip for the top. Butter the pan and line the base and sides with pastry strips, gently pressing the joins together to make a tight seal. Spread a layer of stuffing in the pan and lay some of the poultry and foie gras strips on top. Continue layering until you have 4 layers of stuffing and 3 layers of poultry and foie gras strips. Pierce 4 holes evenly along the length of pastry for the lid, dampen the edges, and lay it over the final layer of stuffing, pressing the edges against the strips lining the sides of the pan to seal. Roll 4 strips of aluminum foil into narrow tubes and insert these into the holes in the pastry lid so they rest on top of the stuffing. They will act as vents for steam to escape during baking. Whisk the egg yolk with the water and brush over the pastry. Bake for 15 minutes, until the crust has browned lightly, and then reduce the oven temperature to 325°F (170°C/Gas mark 3). Bake for an additional 45 minutes until the core temperature of the pie has reached 154°F (68°C). Pour some of the aspic slowly into the pie through the foil vents as it will be absorbed better while the stuffing is hot. Leave the vents in place and let the pie cool, before pouring in the remaining aspic, again through the vents. The aspic should cover the stuffing and come up to the bottom of the vents. Carefully lift them out and let the pie rest for a minimum of 24 hours before serving, to ensure the flavors mature and meld.

TO SERVE

Cut the pâté en croûte into slices and serve with the pickled black chanterelles alongside, garnished with a handful of frisée lettuce, pea shoots, and hazelnuts.

CHEFS' NOTES

Traditionally, a pâté en croûte has 4 layers of stuffing and 3 layers of meat cut into strips.

HEDGEHOG MUSHROOMS WITH MARROW BONE

Pieds-de-mouton et os à moelle

Serves 6

Active time
20 minutes

Cooking time
30 minutes

Equipment
Flower-shaped 1¼-in.
(3-cm) cookie cutter
2 silicone baking mats

Ingredients

Hedgehog mushrooms
1 lb. 5 oz. (600 g)
hedgehog (*pieds de mouton*) mushrooms

½ onion, preferably
pink Roscoff or another
sweet variety

Butter for frying

1 tbsp chopped fresh
parsley

Salt and freshly ground
pepper

Marrow bones
3 marrow bones,
halved lengthwise
by your butcher

Melba toast
3 tbsp (2 oz./50 g)
butter

2 × ¼-in. (5-mm) slices
from a sandwich loaf

Spinach
1 oz. (30 g) baby spinach
leaves

To serve
6 slices pata negra,
or other Spanish cured
ham, cut into smaller
pieces

PREPARING THE MUSHROOMS
Clean, wash, and chop or slice the mushrooms (see technique p. 35). Peel and chop the onion (see technique p. 56). In a skillet over high heat, melt the butter and briefly sauté the mushrooms with the onion. Season with salt and pepper and stir in the chopped parsley.

PREPARING THE MARROW BONES
Carefully clean the bones so they are ready to use for serving. Preheat the oven to 350°F (180°C/Gas mark 4). Place the bones in an ovenproof dish and bake for 10–12 minutes, depending on their size. Remove from the oven and keep warm. Reduce the oven temperature to 325°F (170°C/Gas mark 3).

PREPARING THE MELBA TOAST
Clarify the butter by melting it gently in a heavy saucepan over low heat. Skim off the froth, then pour the clear yellow layer of clarified butter into a jug, leaving behind the milky residue. Using the flower-shaped cookie cutter, cut out 12 flowers from the bread slices and lay them on one of the baking mats. Brush with the clarified butter, place the second baking mat on top, and bake in the oven for 8 minutes.

PREPARING THE BABY SPINACH
Wash and spin dry the baby spinach leaves (see technique p. 28).

TO SERVE
Return the marrow bones to the oven for a few minutes and then spoon the mushrooms on top, reserving a few slices for garnish. Arrange the pata negra slices, baby spinach leaves, reserved mushroom slices, and Melba toast flowers attractively on top.

BLACK TRUFFLE DIAMOND CHAUD-FROID

Diamant truffe noire en chaud-froid

Serves 6

Active time
1 hour

Cooking time
30 minutes

Equipment
Food processor
Fine-mesh sieve
Pastry bag
2-in. (5-cm) round cookie cutter
Truffle brush
Mandoline
Steamer
Blender

Ingredients

Creamy chicken stuffing
5 oz. (150 g) chicken breasts
Scant ¼ cup (1¾ oz./50 g) egg white (about 2 whites)
Scant ½ cup (100 ml) cream, minimum 35% fat
1 tsp (5 ml) squid ink

Potatoes
3 large potatoes
4 tsp (20 ml) truffle oil
3 tbsp (50 ml) white chicken stock
Fleur de sel
Freshly ground pepper

Potato glaze
Scant ½ cup (100 ml) brown chicken *jus*
4 tsp (20 ml) Madeira

Black truffles
6 × 2 oz. (60 g) black truffles
A little truffle oil, for glazing

Truffle vinaigrette
1 egg
1 tbsp (15 g) truffle-scented mustard
4 tsp (20 ml) balsamic vinegar
3 tbsp (50 ml) virgin olive oil
½ tsp Viandox (concentrated meat extract)

Croutons
3½ oz. (100 g) slices from a sandwich loaf
Scant ½ cup (100 ml) peanut oil
Fine sea salt

To serve
7 oz. (200 g) yellow frisée lettuce
1 sheet gold leaf (optional)
¼ bunch chervil

PREPARING THE CREAMY CHICKEN STUFFING

In a food processor, finely chop the chicken breasts with the egg white and cream. Push through a fine-mesh sieve to ensure the texture is very smooth and then stir in the squid ink. Transfer to a pastry bag and refrigerate until needed.

PREPARING THE POTATOES

Boil the unpeeled potatoes. Drain, peel, and cut them into slices just under ½ in. (1 cm) thick. Using the round cookie cutter, cut the slices into disks. Spread the disks in a rimmed baking sheet with the truffle oil and the white chicken stock. Season with fleur de sel and pepper and set aside.

PREPARING THE POTATO GLAZE

In a small heavy saucepan, reduce the brown chicken *jus* with the Madeira wine. Use this sauce to glaze the warm potato disks.

PREPARING THE BLACK TRUFFLES

Clean the truffles by brushing them and then peel them. Using a mandoline, shave into slices under 1/16 in. (1 mm) thick, reserving all the trimmings to make the vinaigrette. Pipe a little chicken stuffing over each slice and then stack the slices with the stuffing to re-form the truffles. Cover with plastic wrap so the truffles keep their shape and steam for 15 minutes. Let cool and remove the plastic wrap. Glaze with a little truffle oil.

PREPARING THE TRUFFLE VINAIGRETTE

Boil the egg for 6 minutes until soft-boiled. Blend with the truffle-scented mustard and truffle trimmings. Add the balsamic vinegar, whisk in the oil, and stir in the Viandox.

PREPARING THE CROUTONS

Cut the bread into ¼-in. (5-mm) dice. Heat the oil in a skillet, fry the croutons until golden all over, and drain on paper towel. Season with salt.

TO SERVE

Wash the frisée lettuce (see technique p. 28) and pick out the smaller leaves. Wash the chervil. Place a glazed potato slice in the center of each serving plate. Toss the frisée lettuce with the vinaigrette and arrange around the potato slice. Cut the truffles in half and place two halves on the potato slice. Decorate with the gold leaf, if using, and scatter the croutons and a few chervil sprigs over the frisée.

PICKLED SHIMEJI MUSHROOMS AND CRISP CHINESE DUMPLINGS

Champignons shimeji au vinaigre, ravioles croustillantes

Serves 10

Active time
2 hours

Standing time
30 minutes

Cooking time
50 minutes

Equipment
Steam oven or steamer
Instant-read thermometer
Thermometer

Ingredients

Quick-pickled mushrooms

5 oz. (150 g) white shimeji mushrooms
5 oz. (150 g) brown shimeji mushrooms
1¼ cups (300 ml) clear brown chicken stock
1 tbsp (15 ml) white wine vinegar
1 pinch of sugar
1 tsp (5 ml) hazelnut oil
Salt

Foie gras (optional)

2 whole lobes duck foie gras
Fine sea salt

Crisp Chinese dumplings

2 chicken breasts
8 large shrimp, peeled and deveined
¼ bunch Thai cilantro
5 scallions
1-in. (3-cm) piece fresh ginger
½ head napa cabbage (Chinese leaves)
20 × 4-in. (10-cm) square Chinese dumpling (wonton) wrappers
1 tsp (5 ml) sesame oil
Fine salt

To serve

A few leaves red-veined cress
4 cups (1 liter) hot clear brown chicken broth

PREPARING THE QUICK-PICKLED MUSHROOMS

Place both types of mushrooms in a saucepan over high heat, add the chicken stock, cover, and bring to a boil. Let boil for 1 minute. Remove from the heat, add the vinegar, sugar, hazelnut oil, and salt, and let cool.

PREPARING THE FOIE GRAS (OPTIONAL)

Bring the foie gras to room temperature. Roll the lobes in the salt, coating them well, and leave for 30 minutes. Rinse and cook in a steamer or steam oven at 150°F (66°C) for about 10 minutes on each side, until the core temperature reaches 115°F (46°C). Let cool, then cut lengthwise into slices about ½ in. (1–1.5 cm) thick. Set aside at room temperature.

PREPARING THE CRISP CHINESE DUMPLINGS

Using a knife, chop the chicken breasts and shrimp very finely. Chop the Thai cilantro and scallions (see technique p. 56). Peel and grate the ginger. Finely slice the napa cabbage leaves, cutting away any coarse stalks, and place in a bowl with salt for 30 minutes to draw out excess water from the leaves. Rinse and drain well. Combine the cabbage, ginger, scallions, cilantro, shrimp, and chicken to make a smooth stuffing. Spoon small mounds in the center of the wrappers, dampen the edges, and fold up like gyoza. Heat a non-stick skillet, add the dumplings in a single layer, and pour over enough water to half-cover them. Add the sesame oil, bring to a simmer, and cook until the water has completely evaporated. Let them brown on one side only.

TO SERVE

Place a slice of foie gras, if using, in each serving bowl with a dumpling, browned side up, to the side. Garnish with the quick-pickled mushrooms and a few red-veined cress leaves. Serve the chicken broth in a glass jug to be poured into the bowls.

CHEFS' NOTES

The foie gras can be omitted from the recipe, if preferred, in which case the quantity of dumplings should be doubled.

SWEETBREAD-FILLED MORELS BRAISED IN SHERRY

Morilles farcies, braisées au Xérès

Serves 6

Active time
1½ hours

Pressing time
1 hour

Cooking time
30 minutes

Equipment
Pastry bag

Ingredients

Morels

36 fresh morel mushrooms

4 cups (1 liter) water

Scant ½ cup (100 ml) white vinegar

2 tsp (10 g) kosher or coarse sea salt

Stuffing

Scant ½ cup (100 ml) white wine vinegar

2 tsp (10 g) kosher or coarse sea salt

12 oz. (350 g) veal sweetbreads

3 tbsp (50 ml) olive oil

3 tbsp (2 oz./50 g) lightly salted butter, divided

7 oz. (200 g) shallots

3½ oz. (100 g) dry-cured ham

5 pink garlic cloves

1 lemon thyme sprig

Scant ½ cup (100 ml) dry sherry (Tio Pepe)

Scant ½ cup (100 ml) brown veal *jus*

Leaves of ½ bunch chervil

Fleur de sel

Freshly ground pepper

To serve

1 stick (3½ oz./100 g) lightly salted butter

1¾ cups (400 ml) brown veal *jus*

½–⅔ cup (100–150 ml) dry sherry

Parmesan shavings

Chopped walnuts

Marigold leaves

PREPARING THE MORELS

Wash the mushrooms and cut off the stems (see technique p. 35). In a saucepan, bring the 4 cups (1 liter) of water to a boil, add the vinegar and salt, and blanch the mushrooms for 30 seconds. This is important as morels cannot be eaten raw and blanching them in this way kills any toxins they might contain. Drain, cool, and refrigerate until needed.

PREPARING THE STUFFING

Bring another saucepan of water to a boil, add the vinegar and salt, and blanch the sweetbreads for at least 10 minutes. Drain, let cool, and remove the skin and fat. Place them between two baking sheets, stand a 2¼-lb. (1-kg) weight on top, and leave for 1 hour to help press out all the water, transferring the sweetbreads to the refrigerator once they have cooled. Cut the sweetbreads into small dice and sear in the olive oil in a skillet over high heat. Add 2 teaspoons (½ oz./10 g) of the butter and cook until lightly browned. Remove from the skillet and drain off the excess fat. Peel and chop the shallots (see technique p. 56). Cut the cured ham into brunoise (see technique p. 60). Peel the garlic, remove the germs, and chop. In the same skillet over medium heat, melt the remaining butter and sweat the shallots, ham, and garlic. Add the leaves from the sprig of lemon thyme, season with salt and pepper, and deglaze with a scant ½ cup (100 ml) of the sherry. Cook until reduced. Add the diced sweetbreads and pour in the veal *jus*. Simmer for about 15 minutes, remove from the heat, and let cool. In the meantime, wash and chop half the chervil and stir into the cooled stuffing. Spoon the stuffing into the pastry bag, snip off the tip, and pipe it into the morels.

TO SERVE

Grease the base of a sauté pan generously with the butter and add the stuffed morels and lemon thyme sprig. Pour in enough veal *jus* to cover the morels and add ½–⅔ cup (100–150 ml) sherry, according to taste. Braise the morels over low heat, basting them regularly with the cooking liquid until glazed. Serve the stuffed morel mushrooms in soup plates with a little cooking liquid, garnished with Parmesan shavings, chopped walnuts, and marigold leaves.

APPENDIXES

INDEX

INDEX (continued)

Acknowledgments

The Publisher wishes to thank all of the teams
who worked enthusiastically on this volume,
in spite of the difficult context: the chefs at the
École FERRANDI Paris, **Jérémie Barnay, Stéphane Jakic,**
and **Frédéric Lesourd,** for their expertise and creativity;
Audrey Janet for her organization and reactivity;
Estérelle Payany for her invaluable knowledge;
Rina Nurra for her astute photographer's eye;
Alice Leroy for showcasing all this hard work with panache;
and the **English edition freelance team** for their diligence
and patience.

The Publisher also extends its thanks to **Marine Mora**
and the **Matfer Bourgeat** group, as well as the store **Mora,**
for the utensils and equipment.

www.matferbourgeat.com
www.mora.fr